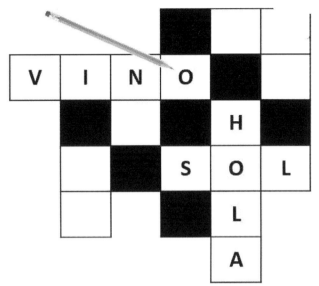

Learn Spanish Vocabulary
Crossword Puzzles - Volume 1

The Fun Way to Enhance Your Spanish Vocabulary

By: Cesar Torreblanca

Other Publications by the Author:

All books created and published by César Torreblanca have one common goal: **To help anyone who is learning Spanish!** Whether you are a beginner or at the point of fluency, you are sure to benefit from their content!

"Learn Spanish *Vocabulary* - Crossword Puzzles"
A **4-Volume series** to help students learn, practice and expand their Spanish **vocabulary**. An Anthology of all **four volumes** is also available.

"Learn Spanish Verbs – Crossword Puzzles"
This series also consists of **four Volumes**. Each with 50 crossword puzzles that will engage students in conjugating over 200 hundred **common verbs**. It deals with the basic verb forms (the ones you will need to get around!)

"Práctica… Práctica… Práctica…!"
These workbooks are a comprehensive collection of practice exercises. Vol. 1 for **Beginners**, Vol. 2 for **Intermediate**, an additional book for **ALL levels**. Also, a fourth book: a handy **Phrasebook** with a corresponding audiobook and e-book.

"Organize Your Work and Learn Smarter"
These journals will help you keep **all your learning notes** in one spot! New words, verb conjugations, expressions, etc. The 'Compact Edition' (9x6 in.) is small in size so you can easily take it with you everywhere. The 'Expanded Edition' (10x8 in.) is larger and offers a little more content.

"The Mega Book of Word Puzzles"
Crosswords, Find-A-Word, Jumbled Words & Letter Drop.
100+ pages of fun and educational material! All to help you practice your Spanish. Answers to all puzzles at the end of the book.

Introduction

You are learning Spanish and that is great!

*This is the updated, revised, and improved series of **"Bilingual Crossword Puzzles"** to benefit **all students** regardless of their level. This new series includes 20 **"Mini Crosswords"**. These are very simple and very short versions of the larger crosswords. Use them as a "warm up" to tackle the larger ones or when time is an issue. You will find 20 of them throughout the book.*

You will find that Across (Horizontal) and Down (Vertical) clues are in English and/or Spanish. On the grid, enter the Spanish word for the English term shown as a clue and viceversa.

*Keep in mind that one word may have different meanings. Write down the one that fits on the grid. You may also notice that some words are in more than one puzzle. This is done to get you to **memorize them more easily**. Repetition is a great and seamless way to remember words!*

***Have fun and enjoy yourself** while you complete the puzzles AND do not forget to write down all new words you come across (on the tables provided towards the end). Look for the two **BONUS** "Find-a-Word" puzzles on pages 65 and 66.*

*Please, drop me a line if you have any comments or suggestions for future publications. This is what sets my workbooks apart from all others: **You can communicate directly with me, the author!** If you have purchased the book from Amazon, **a rating and a comment would be <u>immensely appreciated</u>**!*

I have nothing but best wishes of success for you on your Spanish learning journey. ¡Buena suerte!

César

cesar@torreblanca.ca
www.torreblanca.ca

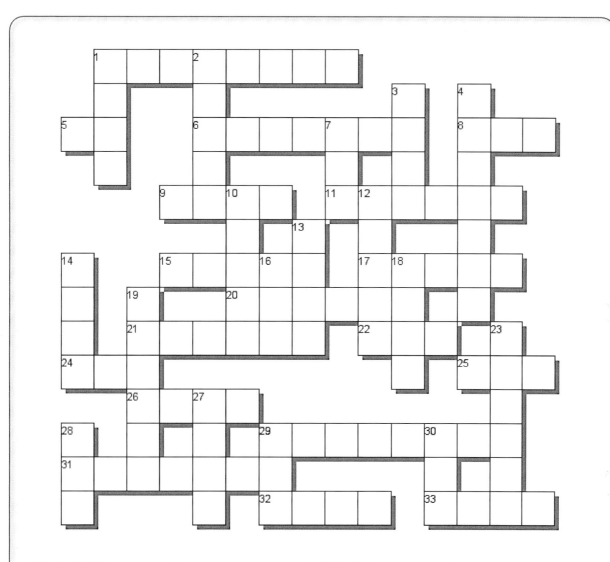

HORIZONTAL
1. deep
5. to go
6. cabaña
8. voice
9. coffee
11. ataque
15. joke
17. noise
20. workshop
21. ocean
22. fin
24. goal
25. guerra
26. ojos
29. lobster
31. angry
32. sal
33. love

VERTICAL
1. but
2. date (in calendar)
3. próximo
4. aguacate
7. wing
10. fleet
12. tres
13. bad
14. droga
16. hombre
18. urn
19. ticket
23. shoe
27. age
28. abeja
29. the (masc. plur.)
30. mar

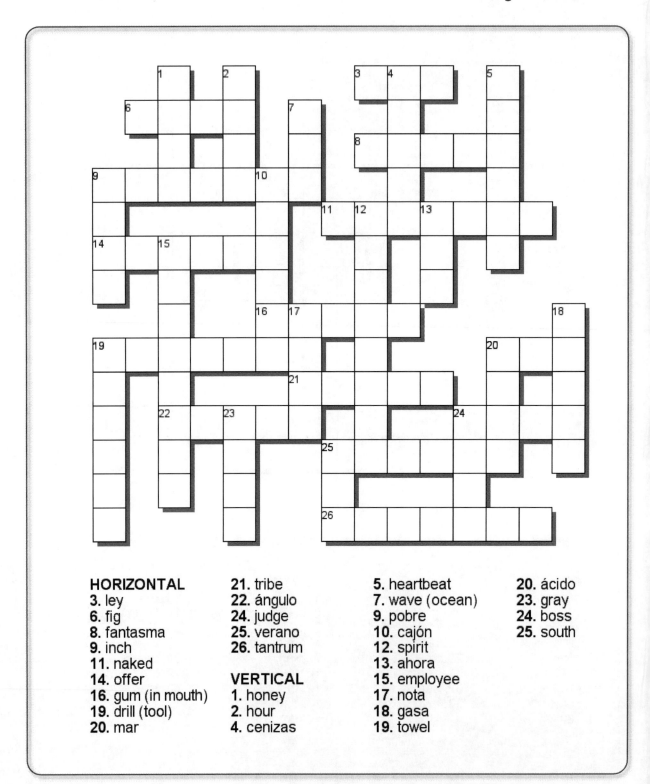

HORIZONTAL
3. ley
6. fig
8. fantasma
9. inch
11. naked
14. offer
16. gum (in mouth)
19. drill (tool)
20. mar

21. tribe
22. ángulo
24. judge
25. verano
26. tantrum

VERTICAL
1. honey
2. hour
4. cenizas

5. heartbeat
7. wave (ocean)
9. pobre
10. cajón
12. spirit
13. ahora
15. employee
17. nota
18. gasa
19. towel

20. ácido
23. gray
24. boss
25. south

Mini #1:

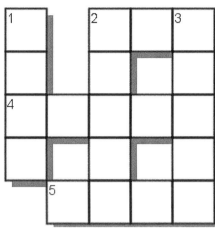

Horizontal
2. apuesta
4. to step on
5. venta

Vertical
1. pipe (to smoke)
2. hem
3. tower

Mini #2:

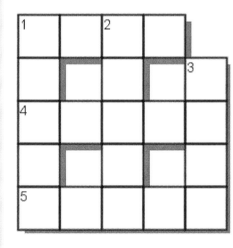

Horizontal
1. amor
4. wastebasket
5. now

Vertical
1. letter (a,b,c)
2. empty
3. note

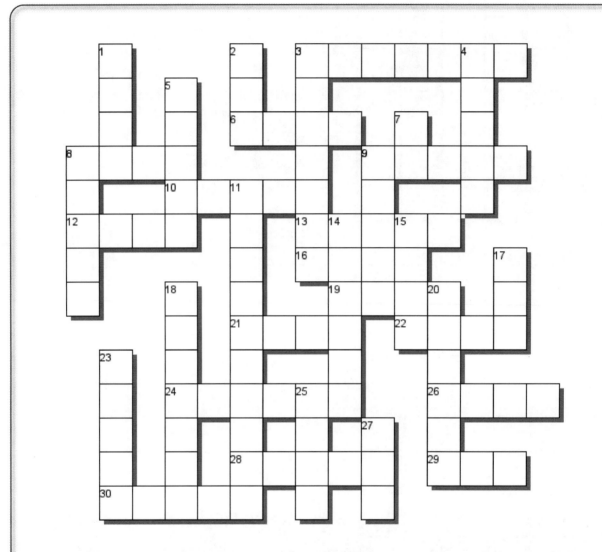

HORIZONTAL
3. function
6. viento
8. calor
9. father
10. to create
12. arco
13. sidewalk
16. lot (land)
19. mismo

21. carne
22. eleven
24. spark
26. descanso
28. long
29. sí
30. hut

VERTICAL
1. caso
2. hilera
3. funeral
4. opera
5. bruja
7. the (fem.sing.)
8. corazón
9. poet
11. stamp (postal)

14. scab
15. oar
17. abeja
18. circle
20. energía
23. magia
25. but
27. sun

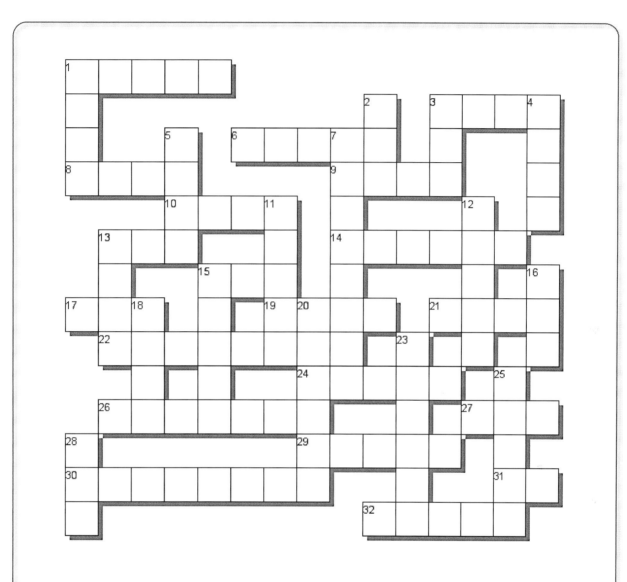

HORIZONTAL
1. olive
3. pájaro
6. strawberry
8. iodine
9. unidad
10. bull
13. aunt
14. trunk (tree)
15. the (fem. plu.)
17. mapa
19. lágrima
21. urn
22. colchón
24. durazno
26. pumpkin
27. one thousand
29. to dry
30. carpet/rug
31. the (fem.sing.)
32. mushroom

VERTICAL
1. solamente
2. hombre
3. pero
4. oscuro
5. boot
7. maleta/valija
11. west
12. bellota
13. equipo
15. letter (a,b,c)
16. impuesto
18. hay (animal feed)
20. wife
23. eighth
25. ice
28. mal

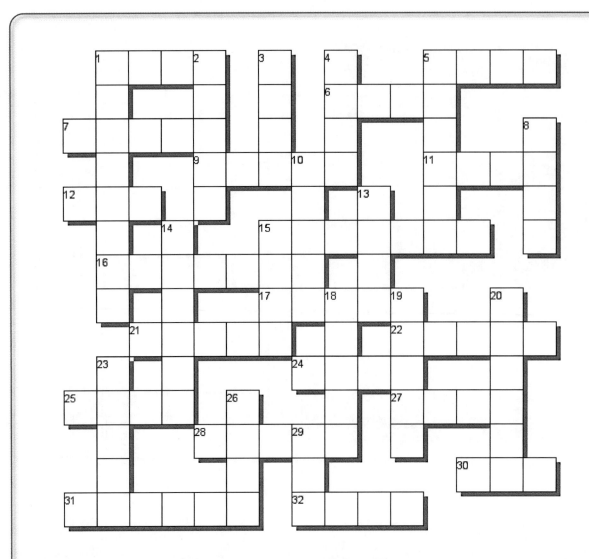

HORIZONTAL
1. pasado
5. carpa
6. east
7. heat
9. octopus
11. wave (radio)
12. abeja
15. lookout (place)
16. drástico

17. limón
21. arroyo
22. odd (number)
24. maple tree
25. que
27. box
28. bruja
30. ahora
31. animal
32. viento

VERTICAL
1. silver (color)
2. clumsy
3. cárcel
4. plaster
5. treasure
8. bathroom
10. precio
13. case
14. zanahoria

15. leche
18. marzo
19. sobrina
20. past
23. espina
26. píldora
29. vaca

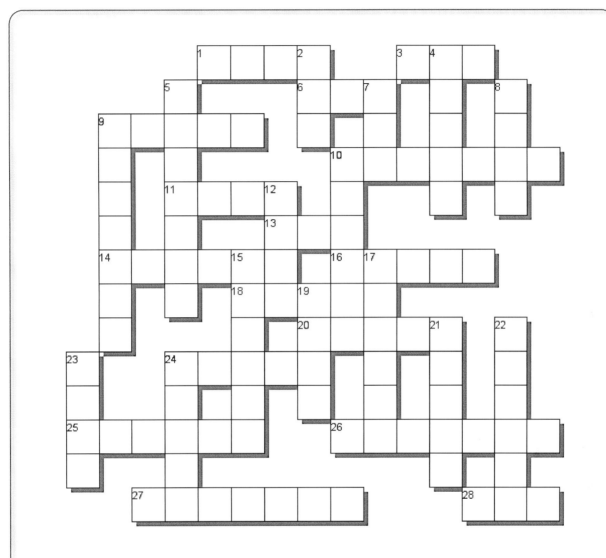

HORIZONTAL
1. flower
3. acto
6. grape
9. spider
10. bottle
11. firewood
13. the (fem. plu.)
14. fondo
16. afternoon/late
18. drawer
20. hasta
24. uva
25. cucumber
26. hummingbird
27. ankle
28. voice

VERTICAL
2. alfombra
4. cidra
5. cookie
7. garlic
8. fabric
9. wire
10. walking cane
12. soul
15. ocean
17. craving
19. judge
21. pencil
22. horn (animal)
23. stern (boat)
24. stew

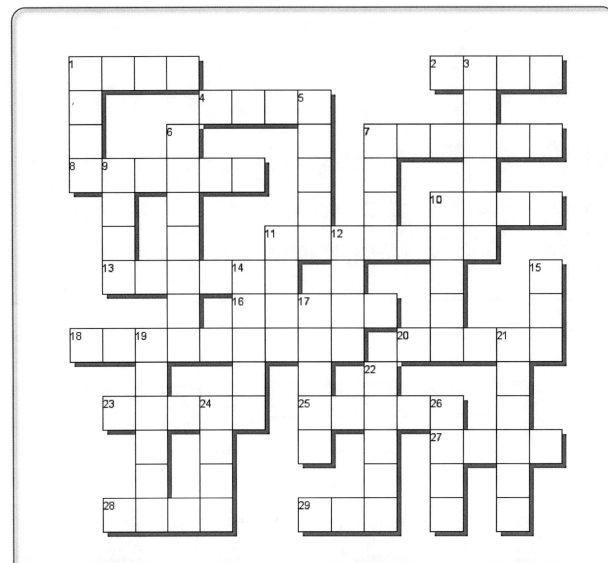

HORIZONTAL
1. solamente
2. love
4. jabón
7. big
8. hug
10. house
11. batería
13. blusa
16. to put in
18. water falls
20. wheat
23. signal
25. tenacious
27. eleven
28. cone
29. zorro

VERTICAL
1. wave (radio)
3. lunes
5. flea
6. soft drink
7. regalo
9. bomba
10. to believe
11. beterraga
12. three
14. pequeño
15. quien
17. tact
19. time
21. Greece
22. índice
24. act
26. zone

Mini #3:

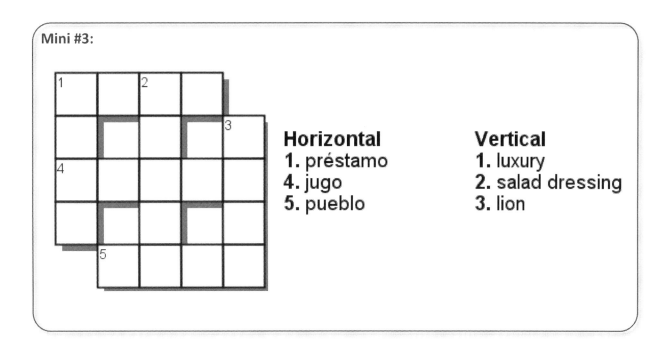

Horizontal
1. préstamo
4. jugo
5. pueblo

Vertical
1. luxury
2. salad dressing
3. lion

Mini #4:

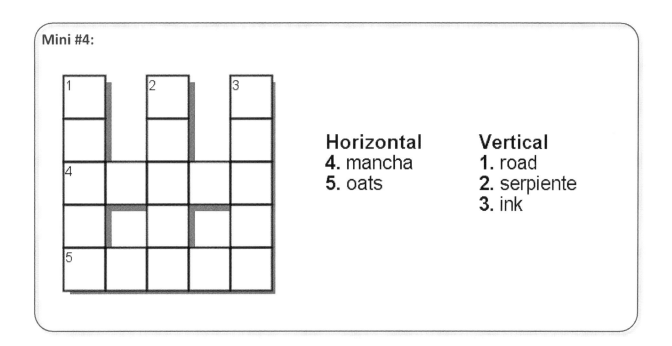

Horizontal
4. mancha
5. oats

Vertical
1. road
2. serpiente
3. ink

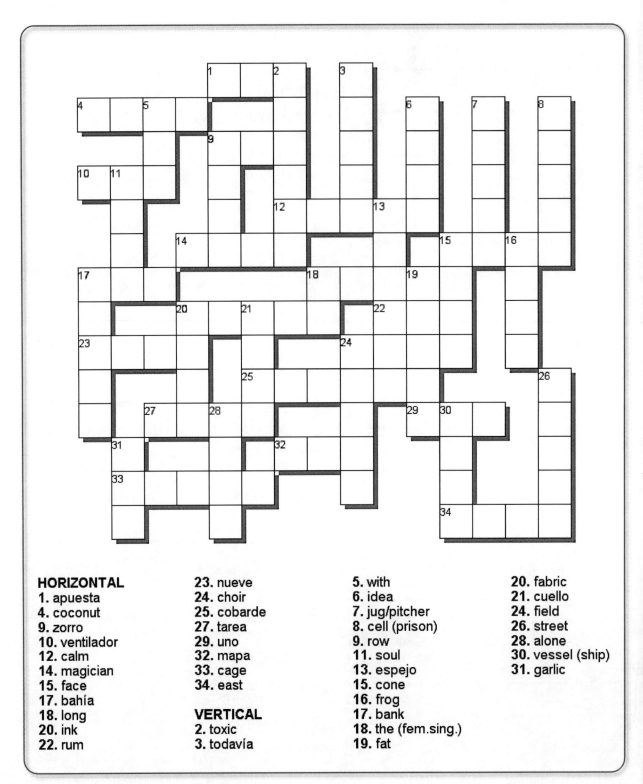

HORIZONTAL
1. apuesta
4. coconut
9. zorro
10. ventilador
12. calm
14. magician
15. face
17. bahía
18. long
20. ink
22. rum
23. nueve
24. choir
25. cobarde
27. tarea
29. uno
32. mapa
33. cage
34. east

VERTICAL
2. toxic
3. todavía
5. with
6. idea
7. jug/pitcher
8. cell (prison)
9. row
11. soul
13. espejo
15. cone
16. frog
17. bank
18. the (fem.sing.)
19. fat
20. fabric
21. cuello
24. field
26. street
28. alone
30. vessel (ship)
31. garlic

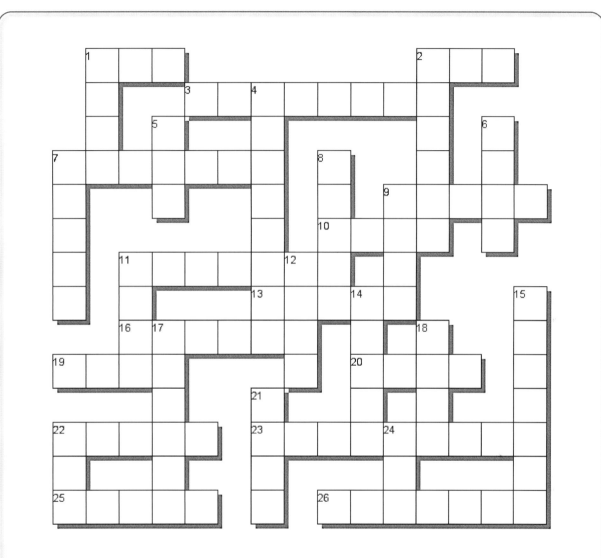

HORIZONTAL
1. vaca
2. voice
3. empleado
7. hummingbird
9. durazno
10. temor
11. backpack
13. paste
16. bolsillo

19. sordo
20. lluvia
22. skilled
23. sneeze
25. woman
26. migraine

VERTICAL
1. case
2. to sell

4. prince
5. seis
6. nape
7. meat
8. eyeglasses
9. leg (animal)
11. map
12. tin can
14. torso
15. handgun

17. oficina
18. león
21. escritorio
22. jamón
24. alfombra

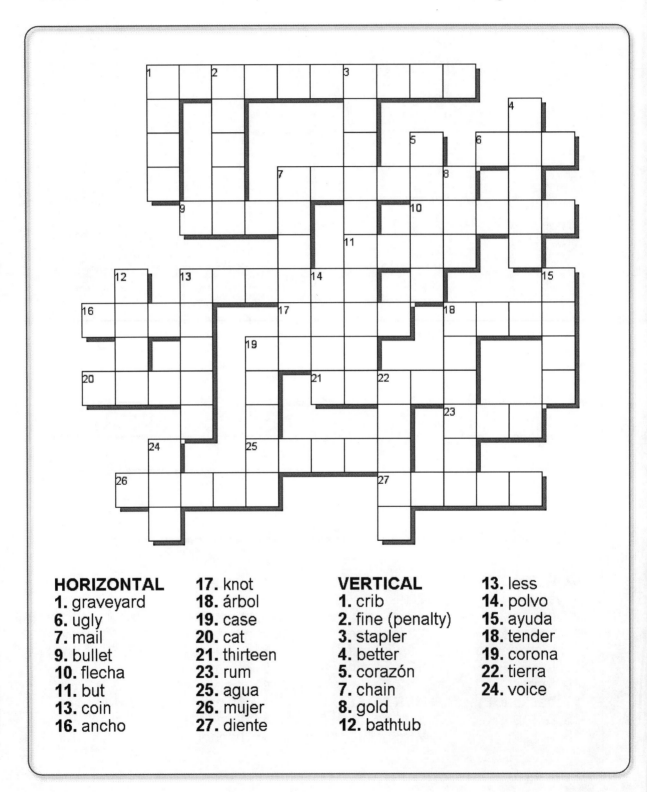

HORIZONTAL
1. graveyard
6. ugly
7. mail
9. bullet
10. flecha
11. but
13. coin
16. ancho
17. knot
18. árbol
19. case
20. cat
21. thirteen
23. rum
25. agua
26. mujer
27. diente

VERTICAL
1. crib
2. fine (penalty)
3. stapler
4. better
5. corazón
7. chain
8. gold
12. bathtub
13. less
14. polvo
15. ayuda
18. tender
19. corona
22. tierra
24. voice

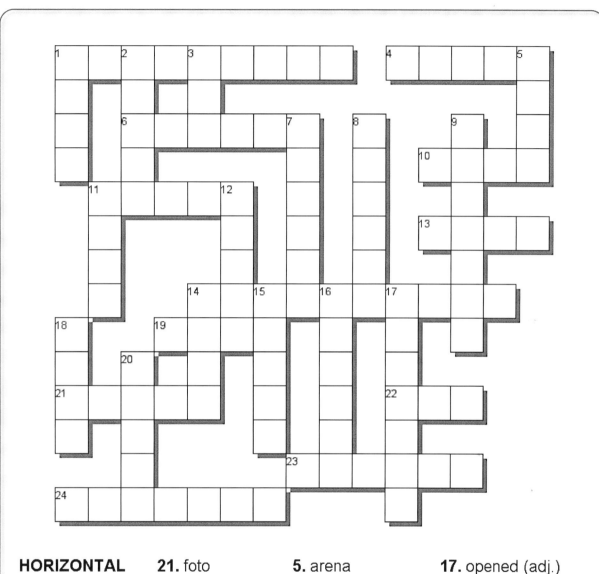

HORIZONTAL
1. cockroach
4. steps
6. abogado
10. pista
11. escoba
13. cinturón
14. photography
19. alambre

21. foto
22. fin
23. hostile
24. martes

VERTICAL
1. each
2. heat
3. hilera

5. arena
7. radish
8. cajón
9. jewelery
11. bathroom
12. older
14. edge (of a knife)
15. key (piano/PC)
16. thick (solid)

17. opened (adj.)
18. potato
20. ruido

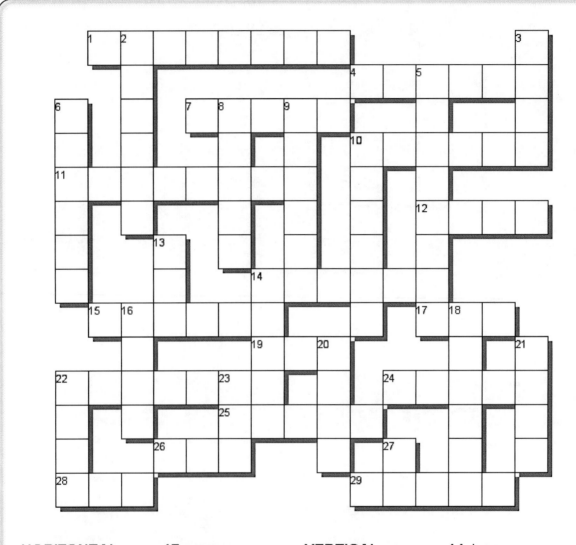

HORIZONTAL
1. chapter
4. fountain
7. marzo
10. tenth
11. ladle
12. tarjeta
14. tub
15. to run
17. rayo
19. hielo
22. savings
24. january
25. range
26. dos
28. uno
29. canoe

VERTICAL
2. ataque
3. kiss
5. to listen
6. ancla
8. to open
9. cinnamon
10. cena
13. even (number)
14. breeze
16. smell
18. accent
20. borde
21. wedding
22. también
23. gold
27. the (fem.sing.)

Mini #5:

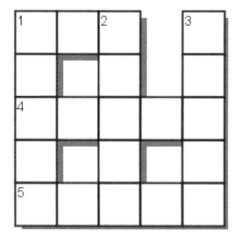

Horizontal
1. perro
4. to hate
5. nickname

Vertical
1. drug
2. scream
3. oven

Mini #6:

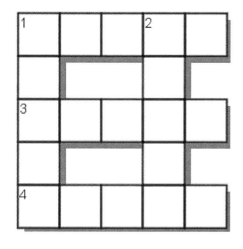

Horizontal
1. full
3. woman
4. to have

Vertical
1. límite
2. nine

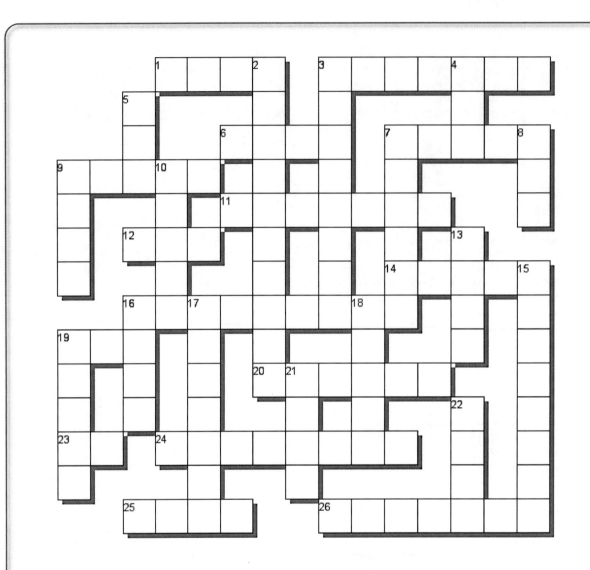

HORIZONTAL
1. barco
3. small
6. pared
7. old
9. seven
11. invoice
12. fin
14. sobrina
16. robin (bird)
19. salt
20. agent
23. to go
24. pregunta
25. ternera
26. tablet

VERTICAL
2. platform
3. politician
4. axle
5. abeja
7. summer
8. aceite
9. venta
10. tenso
13. worse
15. star
16. más
17. texture
18. next to
19. serious
21. drop
22. código

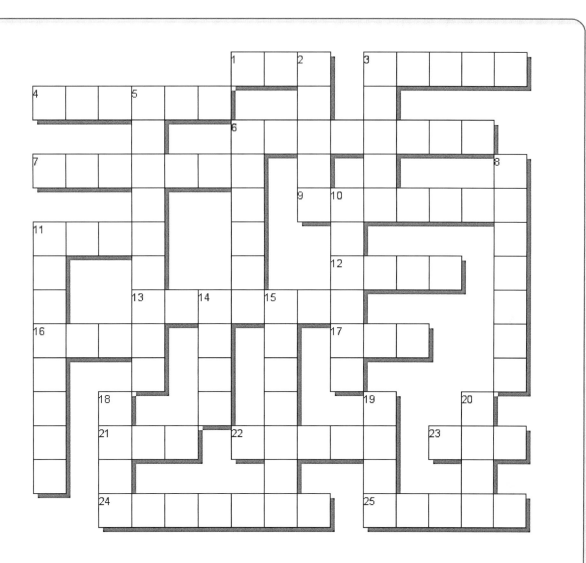

HORIZONTAL
1. costilla
3. hígado
4. trial
6. fuente
7. swimming pool
9. to grab
11. oso
12. something
13. mattress
16. pulgada
17. perro
21. roble
22. oven
23. pierna
24. fork
25. fear

VERTICAL
2. witch
3. letter (a,b,c)
5. cockroach
6. tela
8. first
10. big
11. beater
14. largo
15. beautiful
18. cabra
19. pie
20. kiss

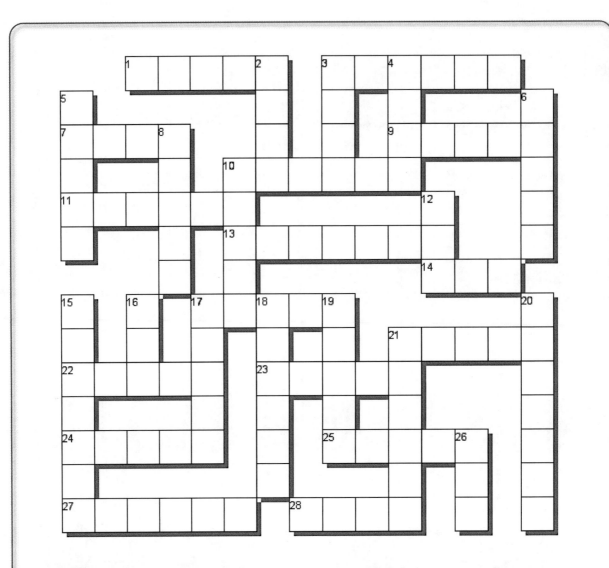

HORIZONTAL
1. cruz
3. blood
7. unidad
9. masa
10. treasure
11. iglesia
13. insult
14. without
17. grueso
21. street
22. crema
23. fried
24. oats
25. tierra
27. accent
28. lake

VERTICAL
2. venta
3. dry
4. knot
5. jugo
6. pecho
8. afternoon/late
10. muslo
12. two
15. spoon
16. centeno
17. grave
18. unfaithful
19. cuchillo
20. lettuce
21. mail
26. jamón

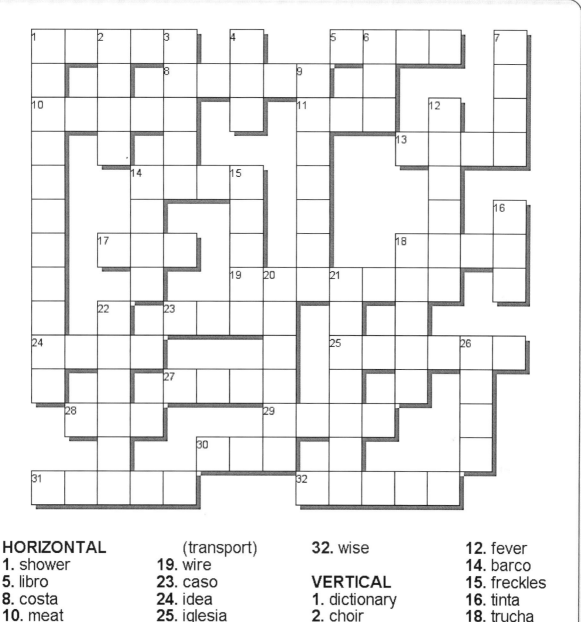

HORIZONTAL
1. shower
5. libro
8. costa
10. meat
11. garlic
13. pájaro
14. jabón
17. aceite
18. train

(transport)
19. wire
23. caso
24. idea
25. iglesia
27. más
28. apuesta
29. hate
30. ventilador
31. levadura

32. wise

VERTICAL
1. dictionary
2. choir
3. steel
4. hombre
6. gold
7. age
9. card

12. fever
14. barco
15. freckles
16. tinta
18. trucha
20. lección
21. backpack
22. cherry
26. almost

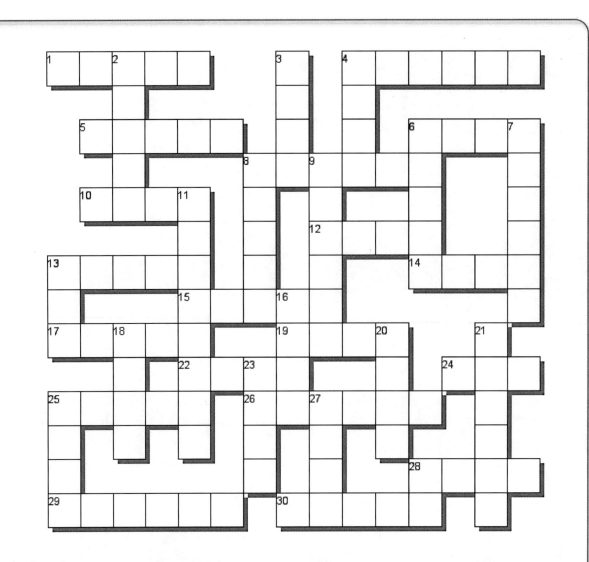

HORIZONTAL
1. eyeglasses
4. pañal
5. ship
6. zapato
8. tomato
10. verbo
12. nombre
13. motor
14. girl
15. escoba
17. paste
19. wolf
22. case
24. pero
25. blind
26. trunk (tree)
28. lot (land)
29. hug
30. cake

VERTICAL
2. marco
3. hiccup
4. dune
6. siete
7. to edit
8. roof
9. minimum
11. barbecue
13. mapa
16. smell
18. semilla
20. eleven
21. port (for ships)
23. estrella
25. face
27. hearing (sense)
28. the (fem.sing.)

Mini #7:

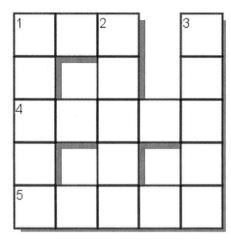

Horizontal
1. pierna
4. cage
5. dream

Vertical
1. far
2. gasa
3. flat

Mini #8:

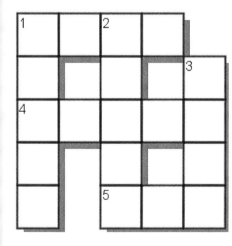

Horizontal
1. descanso
4. widower
5. day

Vertical
1. río
2. calamar
3. hello

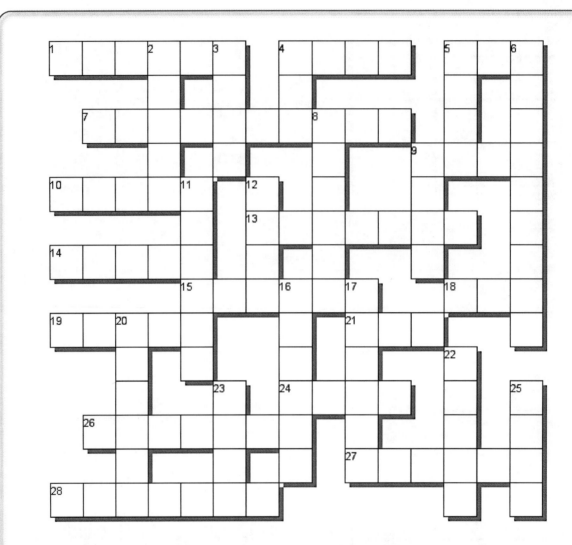

HORIZONTAL
1. to edit
4. eyes
5. alfombra
7. bedroom
9. house
10. tunnel
13. october
14. bench
15. moderno
18. day
19. line
21. garlic
24. celery
26. calidad
27. aguja
28. quality

VERTICAL
2. afternoon/late
3. root
4. gold
5. branch (of a tree)
6. earnings
8. dean (univ.)
9. choir
11. to call
12. bueno
16. rehearsal
17. nación
20. nickel
22. world
23. bathtub
25. cáscara

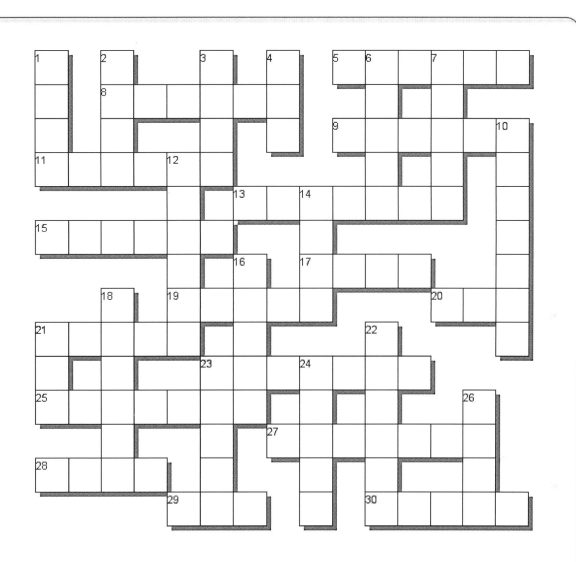

HORIZONTAL
5. angosto
8. broom
9. orbit
11. espuma
13. knuckle
15. trap
17. eyebrow
19. tiburón
20. more
21. ship
23. problema
25. ejemplo
27. horse
28. pie
29. two
30. both

VERTICAL
1. píldora
2. carpa
3. pobre
4. cera
6. april
7. noise
10. anxious
12. thick (liquid)
14. pato
16. father
18. urban
21. abeja
22. barley
23. lead (metal)
24. frijoles
26. monkey

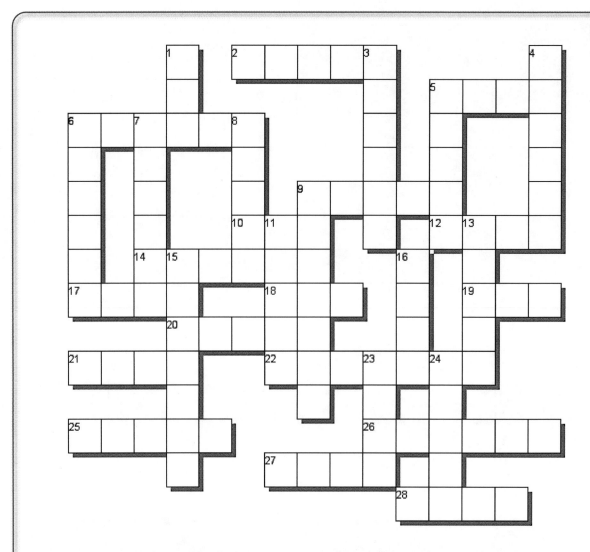

HORIZONTAL

2. game
5. sabio
6. store
9. dye
10. axle
12. lake
14. persona
17. eyes
18. time
19. caja
20. cansado
21. menú
22. fideos
25. easy
26. camarón
27. cuello
28. ejército

VERTICAL

1. bread
3. ocean
4. insurance
5. rueda
6. time
7. team
8. arts
9. fork
11. young
13. both
15. study
16. sello
23. escritorio
24. error

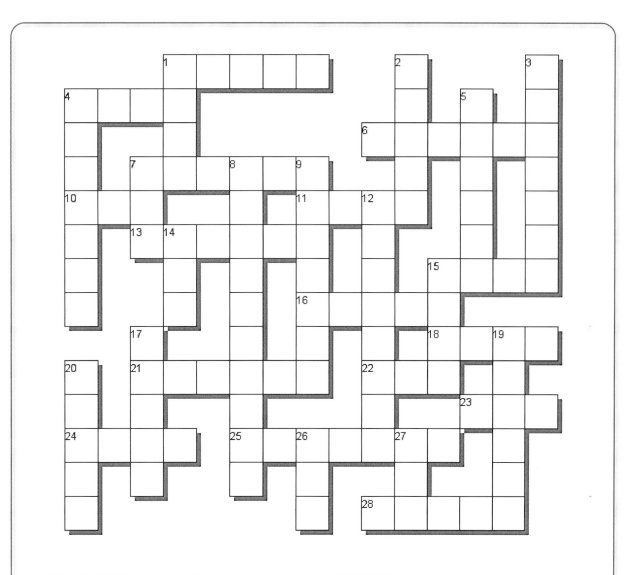

HORIZONTAL
1. hut
4. pineapple
6. future
7. maquillaje
10. fingernail
11. arco
13. profile
15. pie
16. raw
18. efectivo
21. number
22. wing
23. gallina
24. cuello
25. anxious
28. calm

VERTICAL
1. hunting
2. verdad
3. producto
4. stuffed toy
5. fifth
7. mapa
8. sickness
9. palace
12. surgeon
14. axle
15. seal (animal)
17. unique
19. mother-in-law
20. dueño
26. seis
27. mar

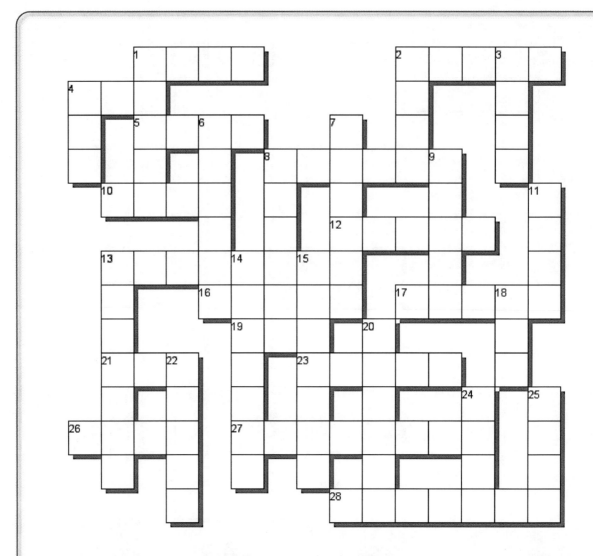

HORIZONTAL
1. mano
2. chicken
4. uncle
5. gray
8. marble
10. droga
12. ancho
13. satellite
16. to add
17. piso
19. goal
21. apuesta
23. to open
26. también
27. guarantee
28. secret

VERTICAL
1. home
2. floor
3. ocioso
4. diez
6. english
7. cajón
8. maximum
9. lethal
11. pobre
13. symbol
14. equipaje
15. drill (tool)
18. bear
20. naranja
22. espina
24. cara
25. hand

Mini #9:

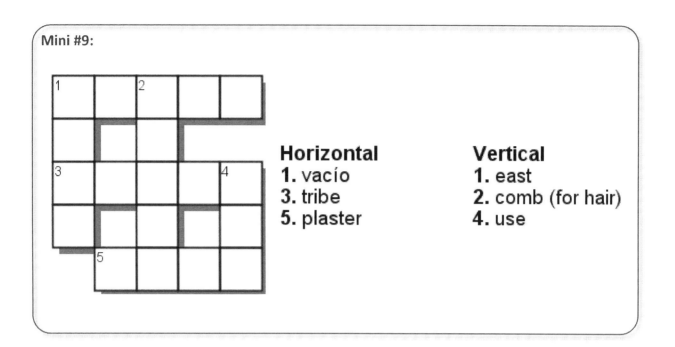

Horizontal
1. vacío
3. tribe
5. plaster

Vertical
1. east
2. comb (for hair)
4. use

Mini #10:

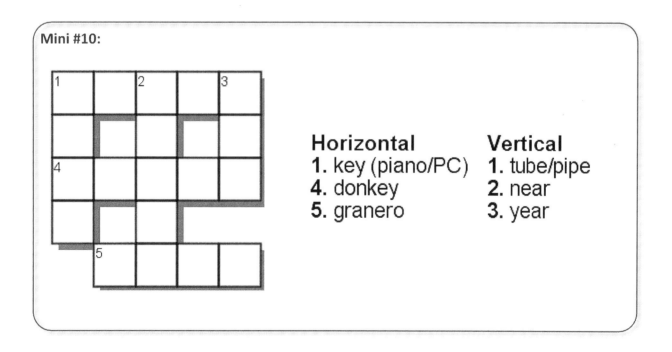

Horizontal
1. key (piano/PC)
4. donkey
5. granero

Vertical
1. tube/pipe
2. near
3. year

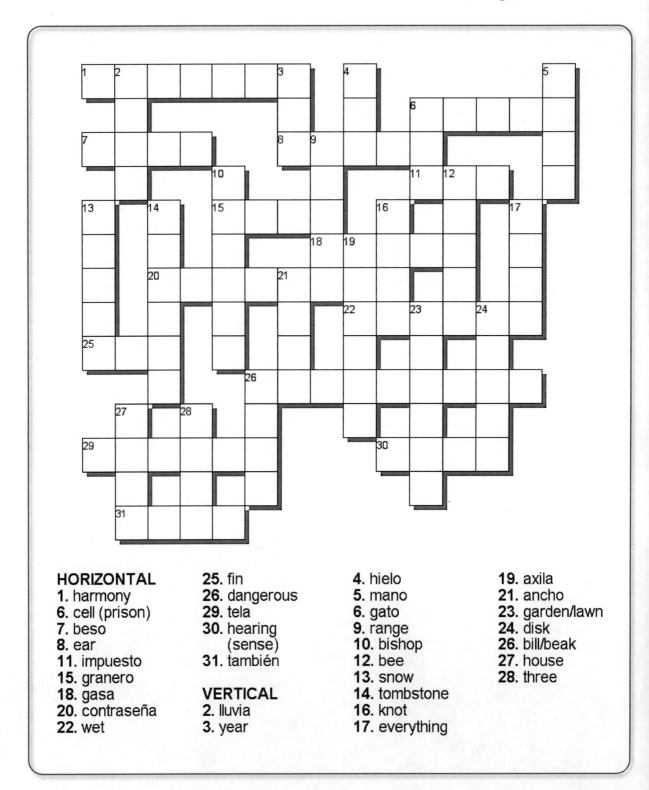

HORIZONTAL
1. harmony
6. cell (prison)
7. beso
8. ear
11. impuesto
15. granero
18. gasa
20. contraseña
22. wet

25. fin
26. dangerous
29. tela
30. hearing
　　(sense)
31. también

VERTICAL
2. lluvia
3. year

4. hielo
5. mano
6. gato
9. range
10. bishop
12. bee
13. snow
14. tombstone
16. knot
17. everything

19. axila
21. ancho
23. garden/lawn
24. disk
26. bill/beak
27. house
28. three

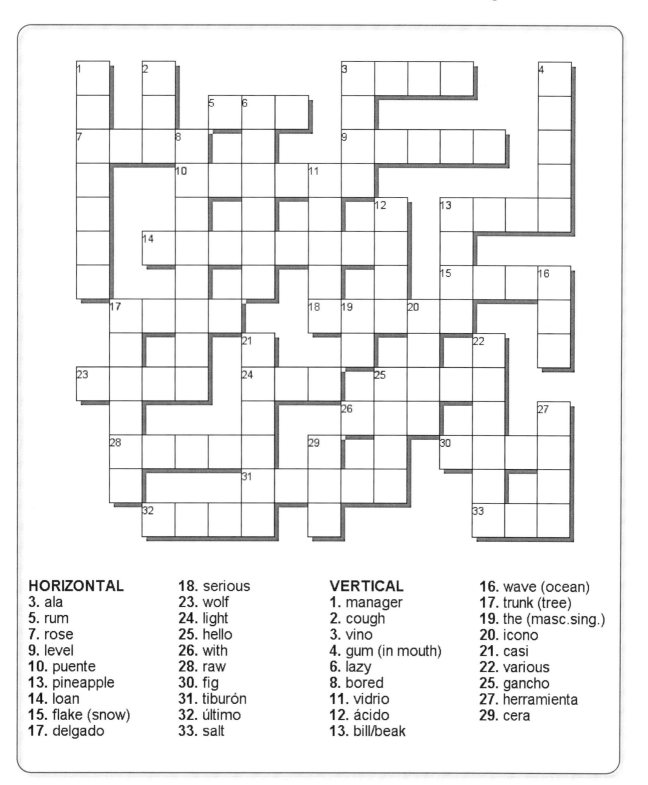

HORIZONTAL
3. ala
5. rum
7. rose
9. level
10. puente
13. pineapple
14. loan
15. flake (snow)
17. delgado

18. serious
23. wolf
24. light
25. hello
26. with
28. raw
30. fig
31. tiburón
32. último
33. salt

VERTICAL
1. manager
2. cough
3. vino
4. gum (in mouth)
6. lazy
8. bored
11. vidrio
12. ácido
13. bill/beak

16. wave (ocean)
17. trunk (tree)
19. the (masc.sing.)
20. icono
21. casi
22. various
25. gancho
27. herramienta
29. cera

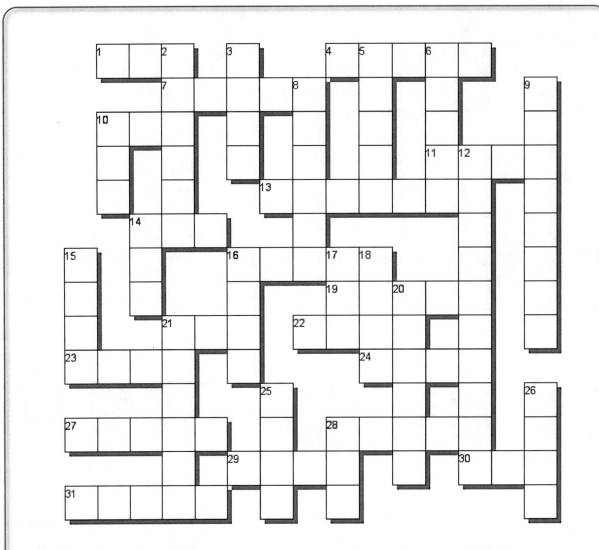

HORIZONTAL
1. quien
4. cousin (fem.)
7. pecho
10. apuesta
11. celery
13. compass
14. vaca
16. corazón
19. mare

21. peluca
22. temor
23. estrella
24. hand
27. pause
28. comb (for hair)
29. moon
30. salt
31. costa

VERTICAL
2. eighth
3. oeste
5. watch
6. metal
8. earth
9. trumpet
10. grande
12. pants
14. with

15. jefe
16. fig
17. centeno
18. equipo
20. free (no charge)
21. muñecas
25. enchufe
26. toro
28. even (number)

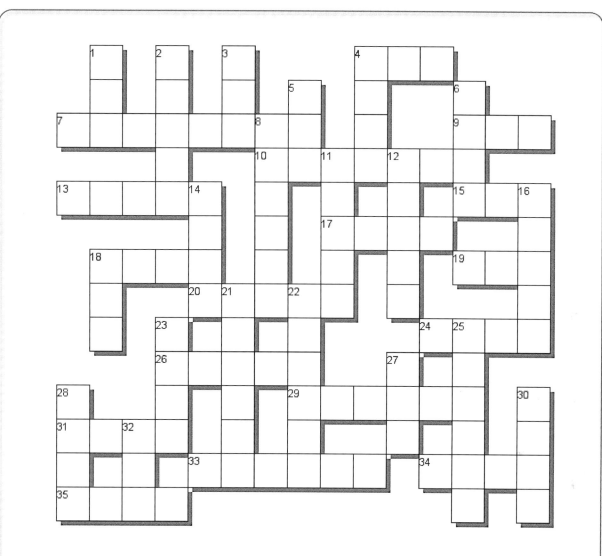

HORIZONTAL
4. abeja
7. cliff
9. huevo
10. sponge
13. tercero
15. pierna
17. ox
18. pear
19. goal
20. marco

24. expensive
26. urbano
29. esfuerzo
31. hello
33. ataque
34. gota
35. nest

VERTICAL
1. fingernail
2. error

3. hijo
4. bathroom
5. cough
6. ternera
8. barley
11. poor
12. granddaughter
14. sordo
16. rooster
18. bread
21. conejo

22. manner
23. sum
25. height
27. with
28. delgado
30. soup
32. tapa

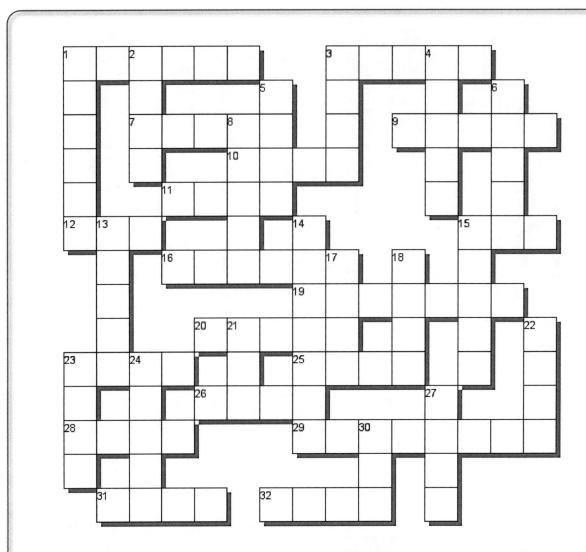

HORIZONTAL
1. bunkbed
3. fuerza
7. hem
9. paper
10. useful
11. wool
12. brazo
15. apuesta
16. almohada
19. grapefruit
20. next to
23. turkey
25. también
26. canción
28. ojos
29. employee
31. palabra
32. root

VERTICAL
1. tombstone
2. tube/pipe
3. faithful
4. grúa
5. datos
6. comb (for hair)
8. tunnel
13. subtraction
14. cabaña
15. to go down
17. lana
18. elbow
21. use
22. weight
23. feet
24. old
27. menos
30. peace

Mini #11:

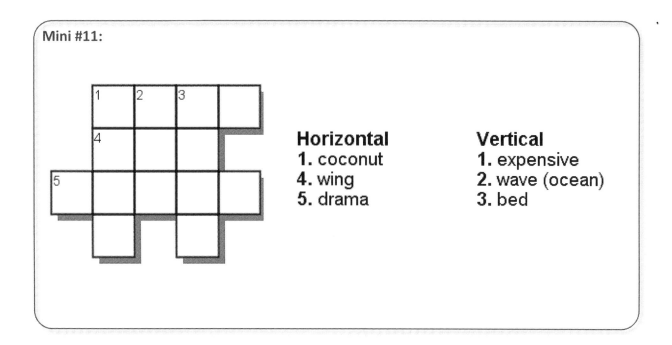

Horizontal
1. coconut
4. wing
5. drama

Vertical
1. expensive
2. wave (ocean)
3. bed

Mini #12:

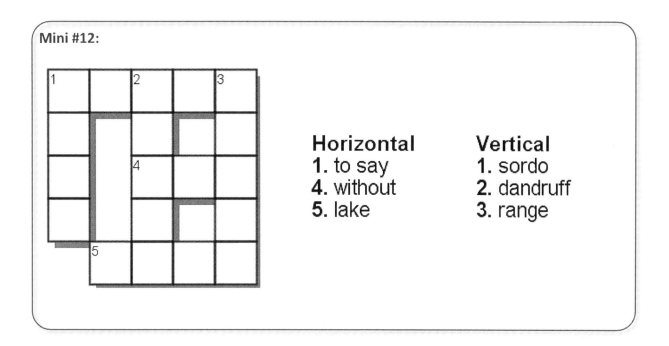

Horizontal
1. to say
4. without
5. lake

Vertical
1. sordo
2. dandruff
3. range

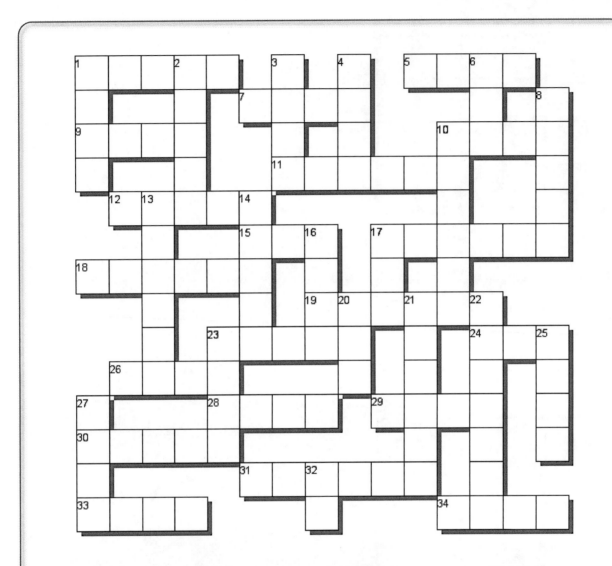

HORIZONTAL
1. sweet
5. ambos
7. wool
9. dry
10. amor
11. medio
12. frijoles
15. cadera
17. craving
18. dozen

19. purchase
23. far
24. the (masc. plur.)
26. choir
28. each
29. urn
30. straight (hair)
31. door
33. lluvia
34. cáscara

VERTICAL
1. polvo
2. hut
3. granja
4. arena
6. uncle
8. black
10. carta
13. shield
14. sombra
16. bill/beak

17. brazo
20. bear
21. leg
22. mayor
(politician)
23. crazy
25. sal
27. smell
32. the (masc.sing.)

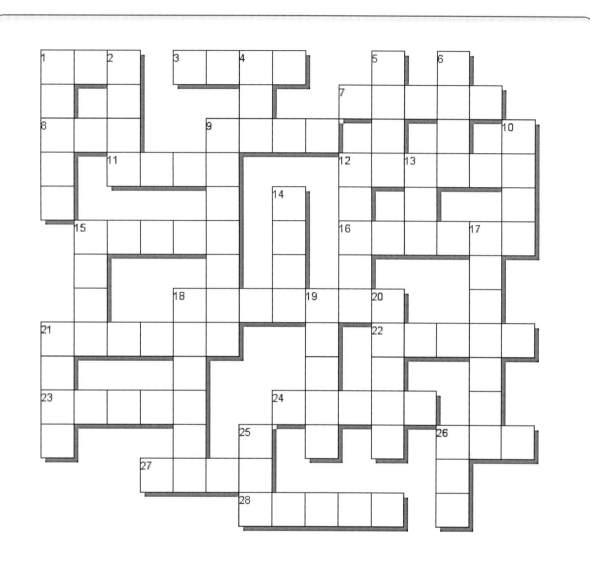

HORIZONTAL
1. thirst
3. polvo
7. nunca
8. grape
9. yesterday
11. faithful
12. tie (score)
15. to doubt
16. gender
18. spicy
21. towel
22. straight (hair)
23. kidney
24. escoba
26. ley
27. cara
28. duke

VERTICAL
1. sur
2. sordo
4. espía
5. equipo
6. finish line
9. allergy
10. but
12. ocho
13. bread
14. idea
15. finger
17. tantrum
18. plant
19. black
20. codo
21. bull
25. rojo
26. tapa

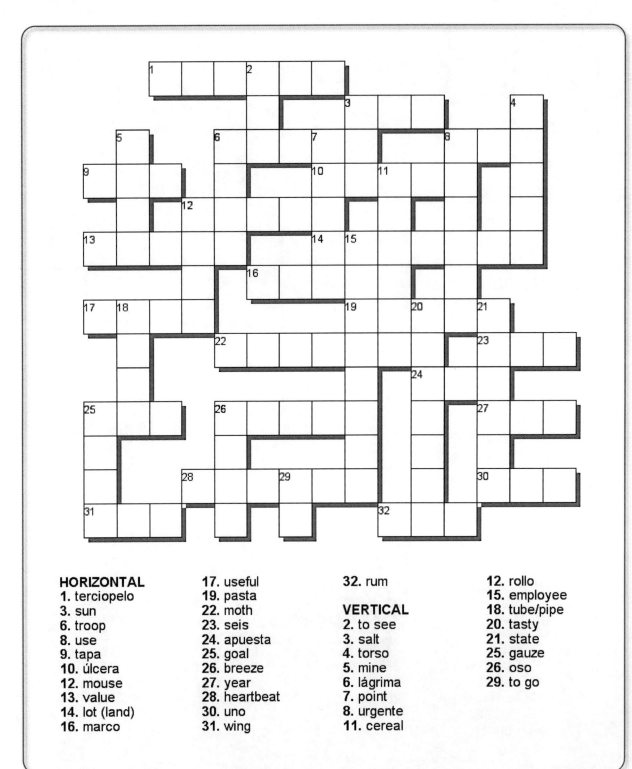

HORIZONTAL
1. terciopelo
3. sun
6. troop
8. use
9. tapa
10. úlcera
12. mouse
13. value
14. lot (land)
16. marco

17. useful
19. pasta
22. moth
23. seis
24. apuesta
25. goal
26. breeze
27. year
28. heartbeat
30. uno
31. wing

32. rum

VERTICAL
2. to see
3. salt
4. torso
5. mine
6. lágrima
7. point
8. urgente
11. cereal

12. rollo
15. employee
18. tube/pipe
20. tasty
21. state
25. gauze
26. oso
29. to go

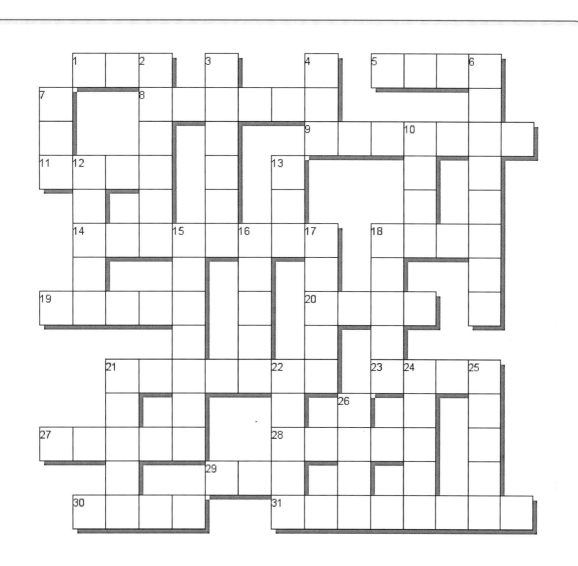

HORIZONTAL
1. trapo
5. tambor
8. clam (shellfish)
9. permit
11. polvo
14. descuento
18. something
19. to believe
20. cuello
21. tracks (footprints)
23. wave (radio)
27. cream
28. grúa
29. sun
30. rope
31. eyeglasses

VERTICAL
2. expenses
3. funnel
4. mapa
6. hongo
7. tapa
10. honey
12. debajo
13. bread
15. race
16. hasta
17. tennis
18. width
21. ice
22. anchor
24. new
25. support
26. pasado

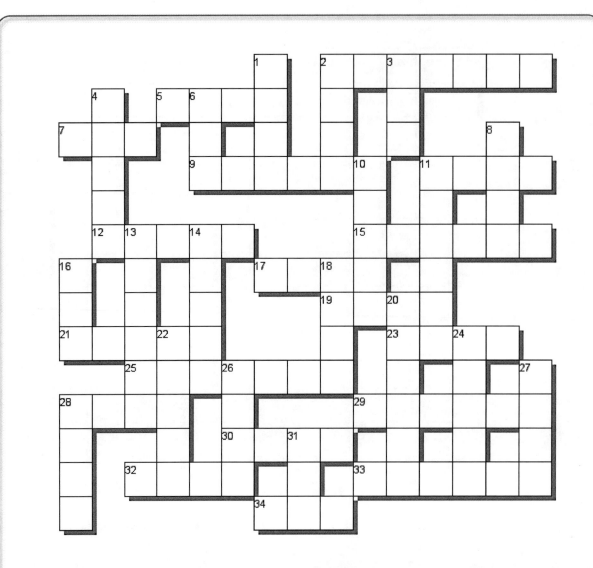

HORIZONTAL
2. punishment
5. idea
7. rum
9. free (no charge)
11. préstamo
12. to have
15. thick (liquid)
17. tubo
19. age
21. silly
23. caso
25. grapefruit
28. flower
29. neighbour
30. escritorio
32. coconut
33. wife
34. jamón

VERTICAL
1. hay (animal feed)
2. almost
3. hijo
4. tostada
6. perro
8. avena
10. velocidad
11. tombstone
13. event
14. error
16. pero
18. scholarship
20. acceso
22. torso
24. Swiss
26. hearing (sense)
27. mouth
28. seal (animal)
31. mar

Mini #13:

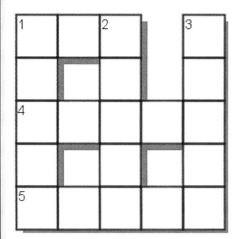

Horizontal
1. aunt
4. straight (hair)
5. spider

Vertical
1. size (clothing)
2. anchor
3. troop

Mini #14:

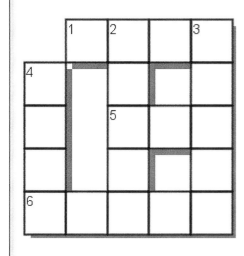

Horizontal
1. último
5. costilla
6. torso

Vertical
2. to open
3. warm
4. texto

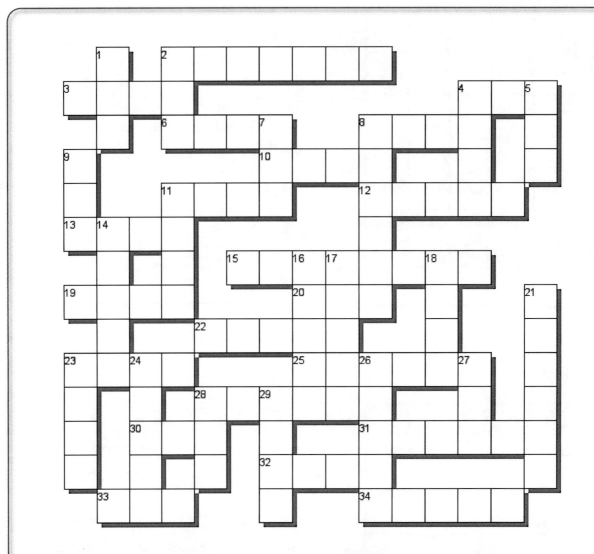

HORIZONTAL
2. compass
3. boss
4. bahía
6. fabric
8. bathroom
10. oar
11. poema
12. silly
13. zone
15. victory
19. egg yolk
20. jamón
22. poder
23. robe
25. customs
28. pañal
30. like this
31. antes
32. gauze
33. rum
34. granddaughter

VERTICAL
1. thirst
2. apuesta
4. bote
5. sí
7. brazo
8. fondo
9. peace
11. potato
14. sheep
16. barato
17. afternoon/late
18. icono
21. bala
23. wedding
24. rag
26. urbano
27. garlic
28. day
29. something

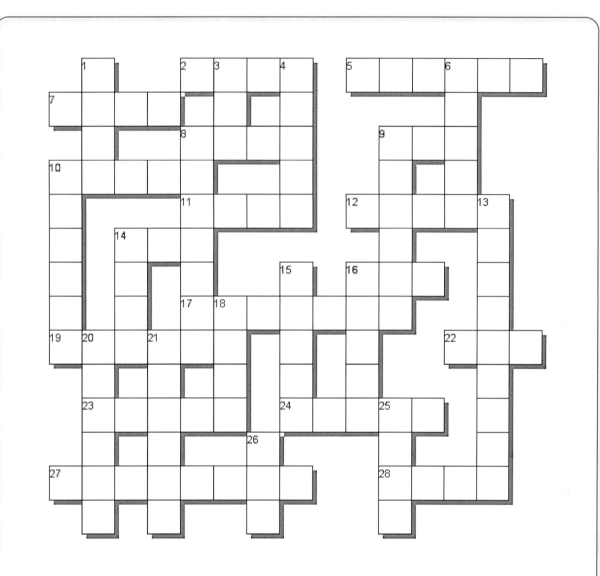

HORIZONTAL
2. alone
5. previous
7. esposa
8. moneda
9. what
10. yard (meas.)
11. nueve
12. watch
14. month
16. time
17. to divide
19. arma
22. without
23. tierra
24. daughter-in-law
27. to declare
28. fist

VERTICAL
1. appointment
3. bear
4. onza
6. old
8. tired
9. to want
10. amarillo
13. gardener
14. mine
15. kidney
16. trip
18. pulgada
20. once
21. morado
25. clothes
26. brecha

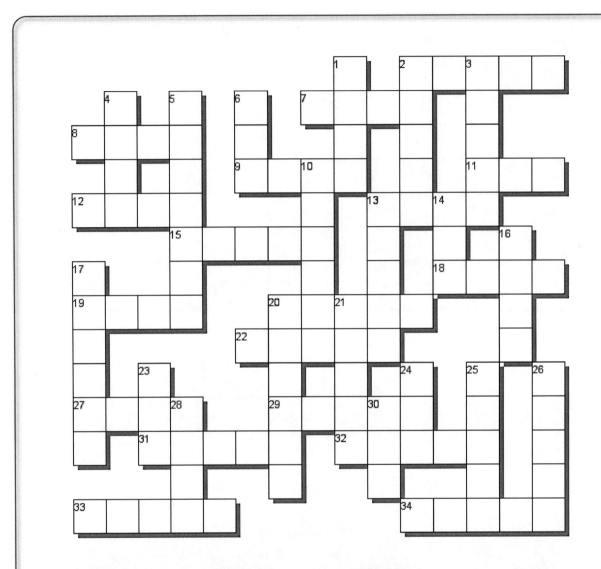

HORIZONTAL
2. wastebasket
7. fuego
8. finish line
9. tubo
11. like this
12. pie
13. gota
15. después
18. to love
19. datos

20. bisagra
22. fight
27. herramienta
29. bone
31. gesture
32. reason
33. breeze
34. cake

VERTICAL
1. vino
2. tenor
3. barato
4. plaster
5. chestnut
6. apuesta
10. barrel
13. drug
14. wave (ocean)
16. bad

17. idiot
20. facts
21. nunca
23. tronco
24. voice
25. to have
26. sidewalk
28. menos
30. salt

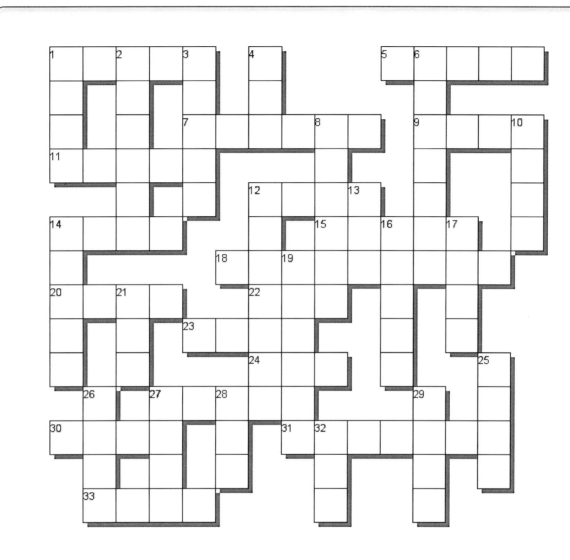

HORIZONTAL
1. barato
5. both
7. bitter
9. canción
11. tocino
12. granja
14. león
15. half
18. stairs
20. toad

22. ventilador
23. madera
24. rojo
27. ache/pain
30. thread
31. opened (adj.)
33. yesterday

VERTICAL
1. cangrejo
2. effect

3. flat
4. wing
6. to show
8. alemán
10. cabra
12. matchstick
13. one thousand
14. ready
16. fear
17. harm
19. hip

21. peace
25. pie
26. bathtub
27. twelve
28. pierna
29. maple tree
32. apuesta

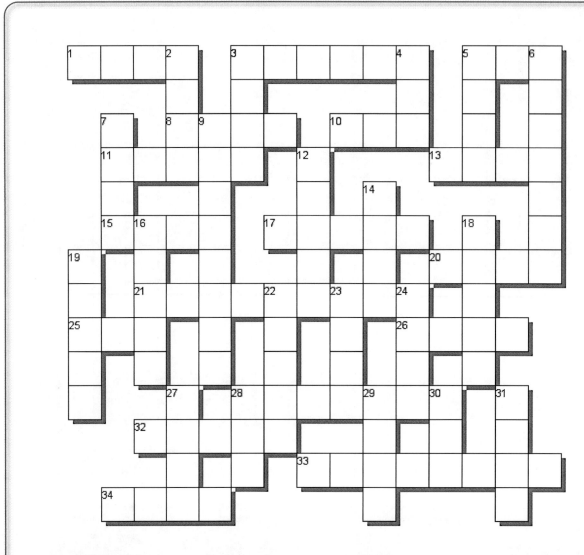

HORIZONTAL
1. cabeza
3. big
5. mal
8. polvo
10. foot
11. now
13. ayuda
15. eleven
17. índice
20. menos

21. document
25. day
26. face
28. colander
32. far
33. accidente
34. palabra

VERTICAL
2. finger
3. gauze

4. axle
5. azul
6. after
7. payment
9. urgency
12. people
14. carne
16. to swim
18. letter (a,b,c)
19. to ask for
22. less

23. nothing
24. eight
27. oso
28. vaca
29. twelve
30. rojo
31. wine

Mini #15:

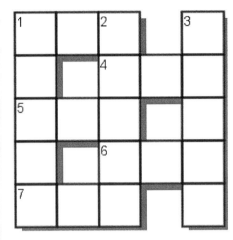

Horizontal
1. with
4. hielo
5. centeno
6. cough
7. bear

Vertical
1. circus
2. grandson
3. tenso

Mini #16:

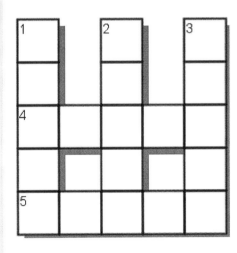

Horizontal
4. clumsy
5. egg

Vertical
1. bruja
2. green
3. bone

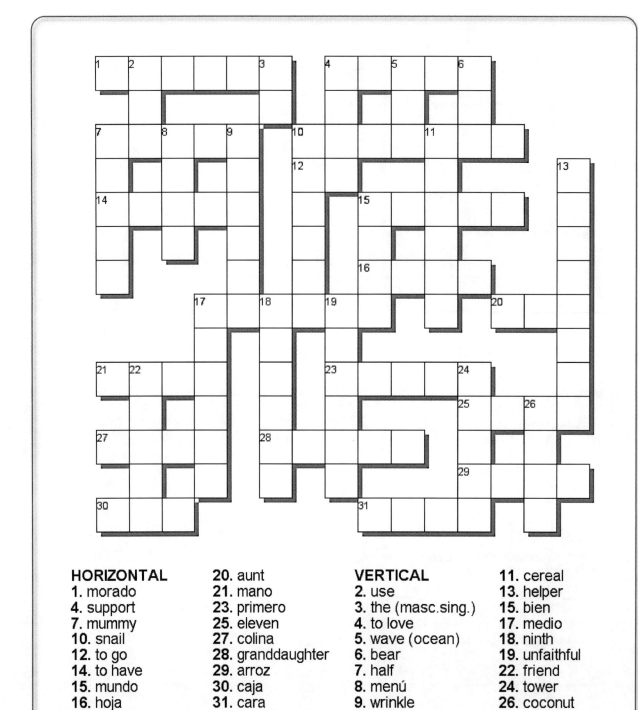

HORIZONTAL
1. morado
4. support
7. mummy
10. snail
12. to go
14. to have
15. mundo
16. hoja
17. apron
20. aunt
21. mano
23. primero
25. eleven
27. colina
28. granddaughter
29. arroz
30. caja
31. cara

VERTICAL
2. use
3. the (masc.sing.)
4. to love
5. wave (ocean)
6. bear
7. half
8. menú
9. wrinkle
10. city
11. cereal
13. helper
15. bien
17. medio
18. ninth
19. unfaithful
22. friend
24. tower
26. coconut

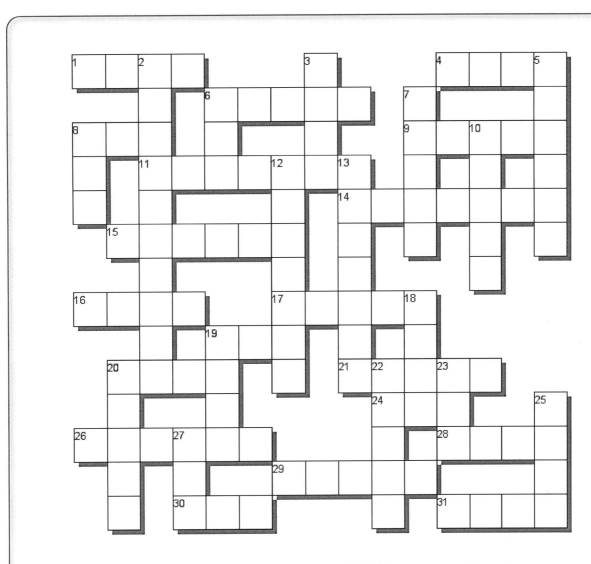

HORIZONTAL
1. pulgada
4. boat
6. watch
8. without
9. ángulo
11. tablet
14. recibo
15. hip
16. judge
17. freckles
19. sun
20. cup
21. phase
24. wave (ocean)
26. origin
28. red
29. cenizas
30. peace
31. estrella

VERTICAL
2. password
3. pie
5. effect
6. costilla
7. brand name
8. tímido
10. scream
12. ejemplo
13. artículo
18. sello
19. venta
20. tres
22. torre
23. even (number)
25. cuatro
27. brecha

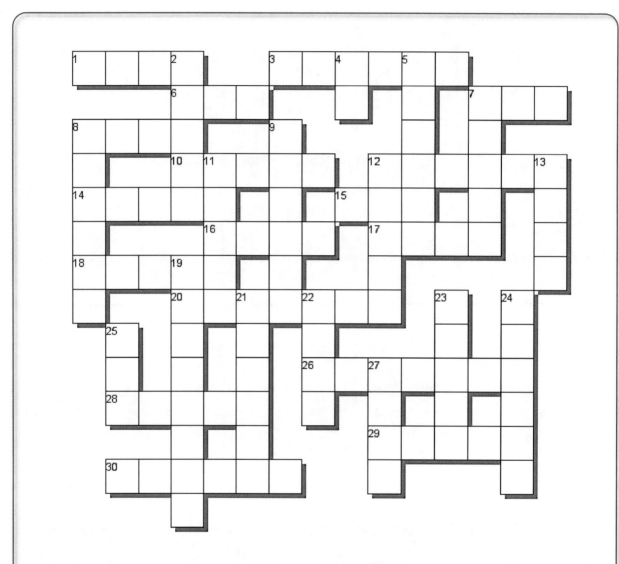

HORIZONTAL
1. rey
3. queso
6. year
7. tapa
8. mitad
10. bellota
12. change
14. bag

15. ventilador
16. oar
17. lot (land)
18. torre
20. still
26. vinegar
28. needle
29. afternoon/late
30. nación

VERTICAL
2. eyeglasses
4. the (masc.sing.)
5. basement
7. free
8. habit
9. trap
11. car
12. calm

13. wave (radio)
19. label
21. under
22. alive
23. to pay
24. goods
25. day
27. nota

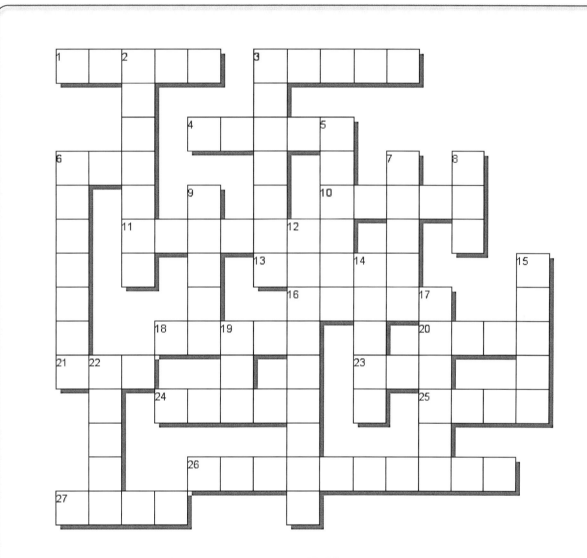

HORIZONTAL
1. milk
3. fear
4. vapor
6. even (number)
10. snow
11. proyecto
13. ground
16. egg white

18. mes
20. one hundred
21. huevo
23. hielo
24. torre
25. nothing
26. misterioso
27. cerveza

VERTICAL
2. corrupto
3. furniture
5. tablecloth
6. spicy
7. better
8. mar
9. fat
12. teaspoon

14. straight (hair)
15. canoe
17. accent
19. nuevo
22. people

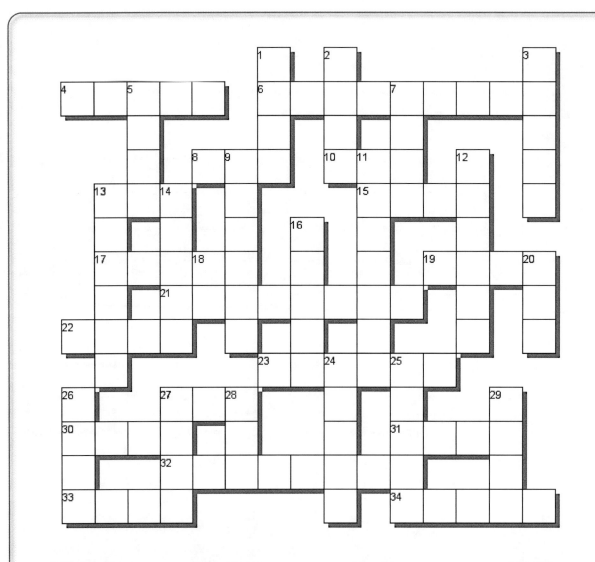

HORIZONTAL
4. sobrio
6. adaptor
8. use
10. axle
13. mapa
15. wave (radio)
17. seal (office)
19. arco
21. baker
22. luxury
23. urban
27. dos
30. tin can
31. glass (to drink)
32. presión
33. drop
34. noise

VERTICAL
1. duck
2. liebre
3. uva
5. mouth
7. train (transport)
9. segundo
11. jewelery
12. tela
13. mezquita
14. octopus
16. to doubt
18. the (fem.sing.)
20. gallina
24. ship
25. nunca
26. bandera
27. lid
28. uno
29. palabra

Mini #17

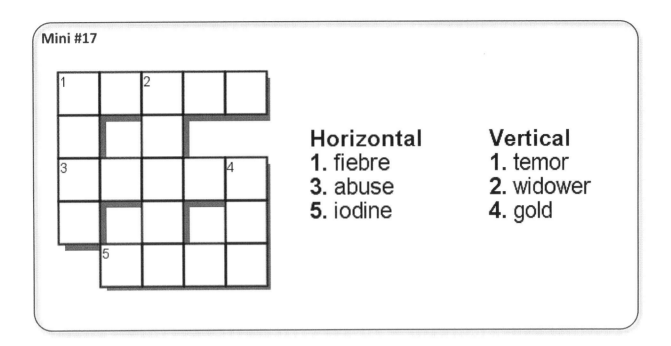

Horizontal
1. fiebre
3. abuse
5. iodine

Vertical
1. temor
2. widower
4. gold

Mini #18:

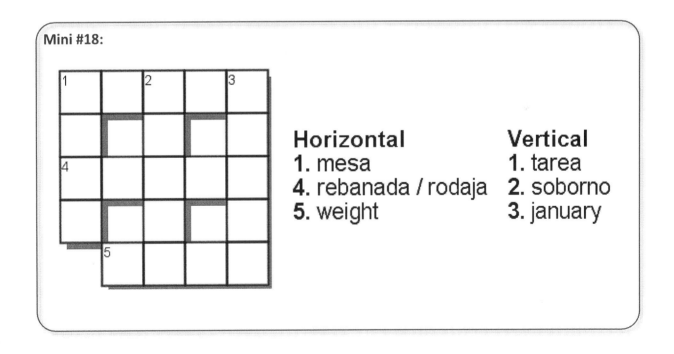

Horizontal
1. mesa
4. rebanada / rodaja
5. weight

Vertical
1. tarea
2. soborno
3. january

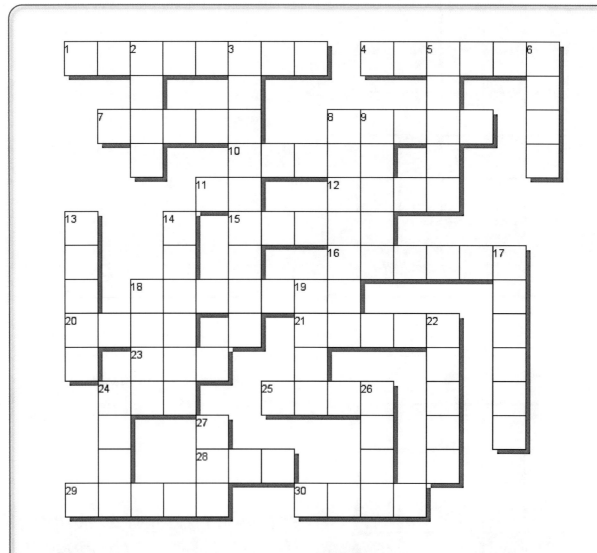

HORIZONTAL
1. alérgico
4. change
7. wall
8. grass
10. favour
11. the (fem.sing.)
12. sello
15. tren
16. neighborhood
18. mineral
20. feet
21. less
23. juguete
24. bread
25. gray
28. brazo
29. mujer
30. carpa

VERTICAL
2. gotera
3. padrino
5. metal
6. hate
8. possible
9. sand
13. field
14. prisión
17. objeto
18. finish line
19. to love
22. health
24. well (water)
26. piel
27. ventilador

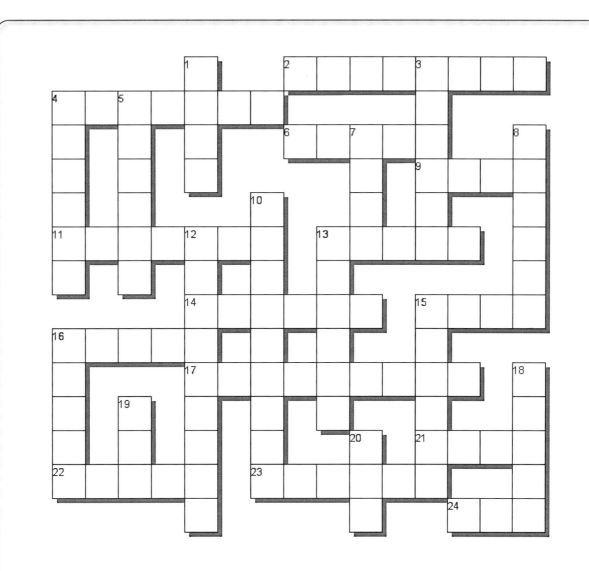

HORIZONTAL
2. washing machine
4. alguien
6. pound
9. bow (boat)
11. backpack
13. black
14. affection
15. box
16. después
17. nurse
21. zona
22. ángel
23. lather
24. mapa

VERTICAL
1. bota
3. pañal
4. camarón
5. doll
7. boat
8. stain
10. sacrificio
12. incredible
13. nanny
15. cherry
16. sand
18. barato
19. perro
20. south

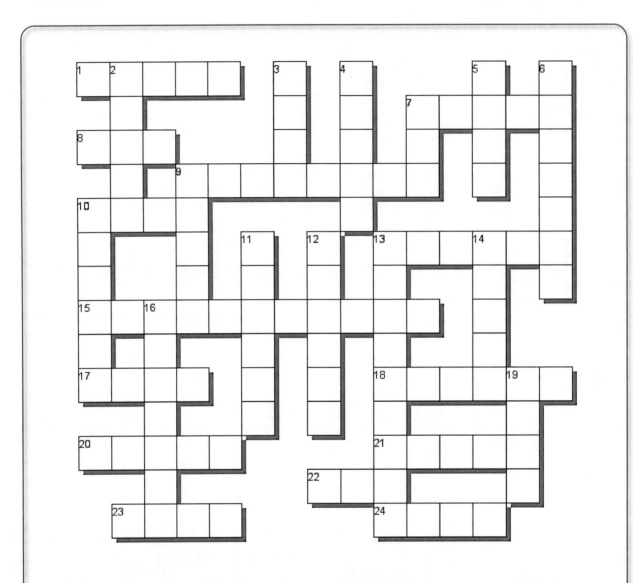

HORIZONTAL
1. april
7. pause
8. what
9. to publish
10. cup
13. axila
15. budget
17. oral
18. summer
20. calamar
21. since
22. mar
23. train
(transport)
24. tambor

VERTICAL
2. blouse
3. cárcel
4. precio
5. cube
6. tantrum
7. even (number)
9. steps
10. temple
11. to blow
12. párpado
13. activity
14. paste
16. to evacuate
19. nut (food)

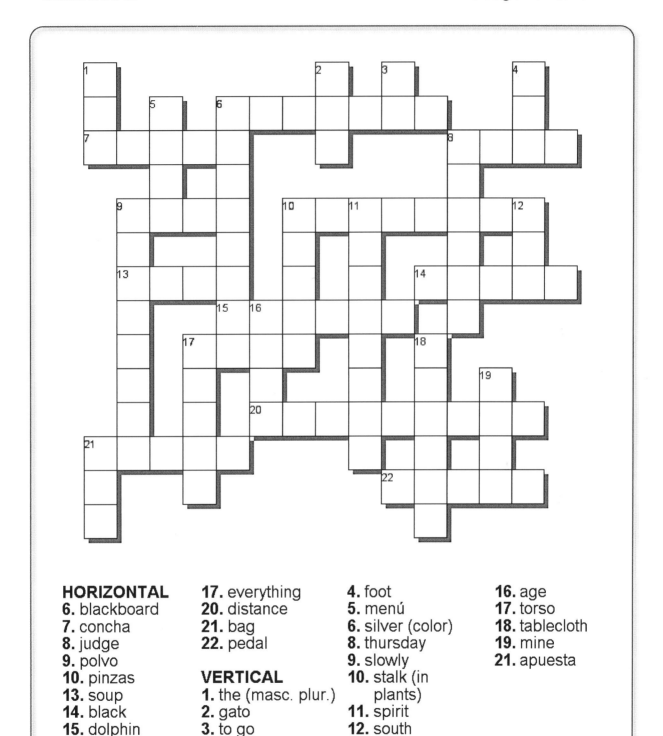

HORIZONTAL
6. blackboard
7. concha
8. judge
9. polvo
10. pinzas
13. soup
14. black
15. dolphin

17. everything
20. distance
21. bag
22. pedal

VERTICAL
1. the (masc. plur.)
2. gato
3. to go

4. foot
5. menú
6. silver (color)
8. thursday
9. slowly
10. stalk (in plants)
11. spirit
12. south

16. age
17. torso
18. tablecloth
19. mine
21. apuesta

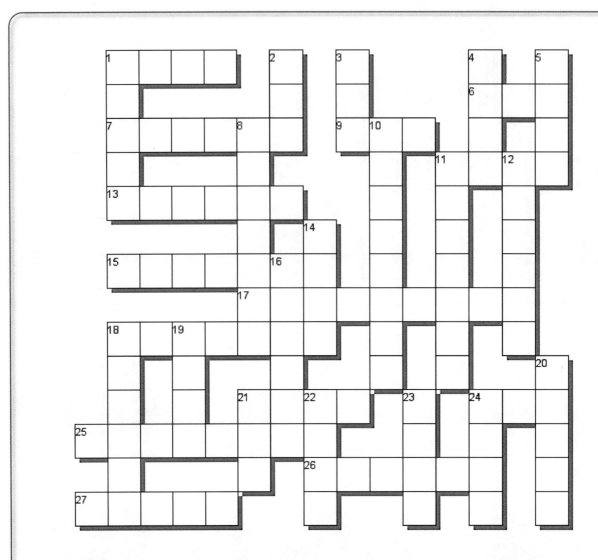

HORIZONTAL
1. almost
6. gold
7. lather
9. the (fem. plu.)
11. cara
13. toxic
15. tear
17. blender
18. spoon
21. soga
24. caliente
25. yeast
26. pantalla
27. durazno

VERTICAL
1. pecho
2. fingernail
3. goal
4. wedding
5. zona
8. backpack
10. blueberry
11. fábrica
12. cereal
14. cow
16. espejo
18. queso
19. crib
20. pasos
21. alfombra
22. pasado
23. cerveza
24. mano

Mini #19:

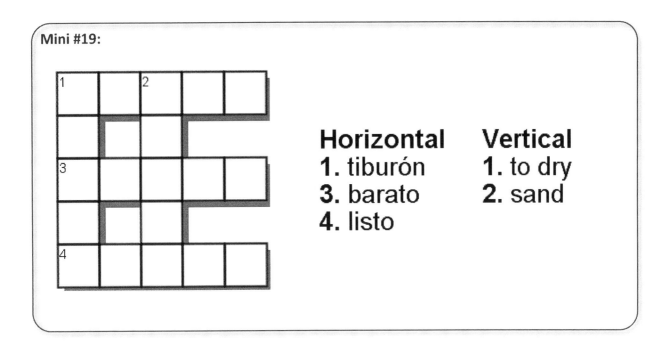

Horizontal
1. tiburón
3. barato
4. listo

Vertical
1. to dry
2. sand

Mini #20:

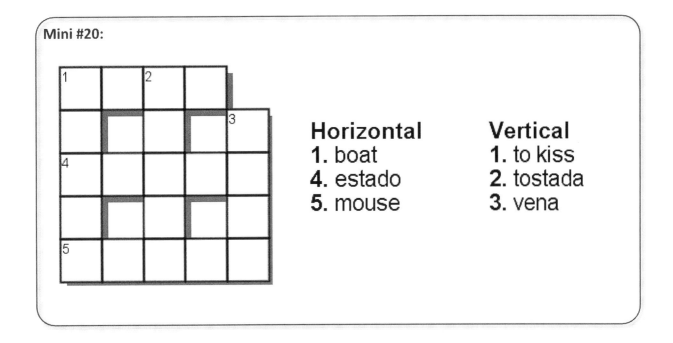

Horizontal
1. boat
4. estado
5. mouse

Vertical
1. to kiss
2. tostada
3. vena

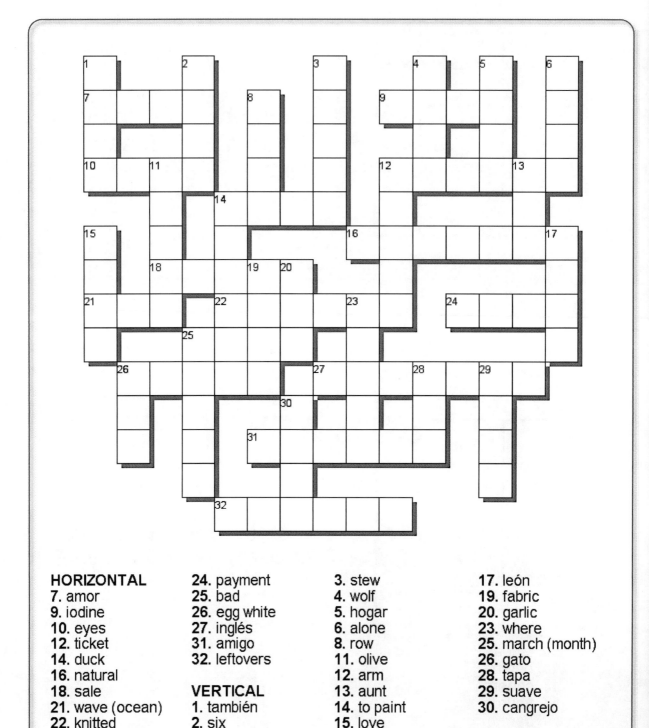

HORIZONTAL
7. amor
9. iodine
10. eyes
12. ticket
14. duck
16. natural
18. sale
21. wave (ocean)
22. knitted

24. payment
25. bad
26. egg white
27. inglés
31. amigo
32. leftovers

VERTICAL
1. también
2. six

3. stew
4. wolf
5. hogar
6. alone
8. row
11. olive
12. arm
13. aunt
14. to paint
15. love

17. león
19. fabric
20. garlic
23. where
25. march (month)
26. gato
28. tapa
29. suave
30. cangrejo

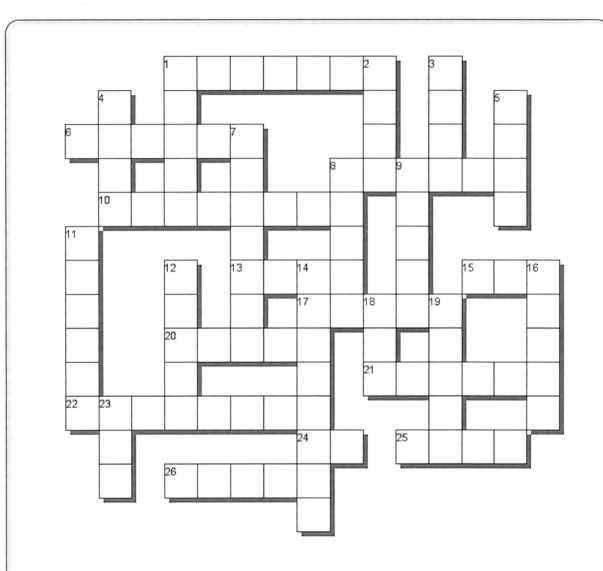

HORIZONTAL
1. hipo
6. hip
8. theory
10. leopard
13. beterraga
15. cadera
17. tiburón
20. barato
21. origin
22. to write
24. to go
25. escritorio
26. noche

VERTICAL
1. hole
2. tamaño
3. love
4. pared
5. gotera
7. wire
8. diente
9. dueño
11. park
12. to take out
14. spirit
16. comb (for hair)
18. year
19. cuchillo
23. without

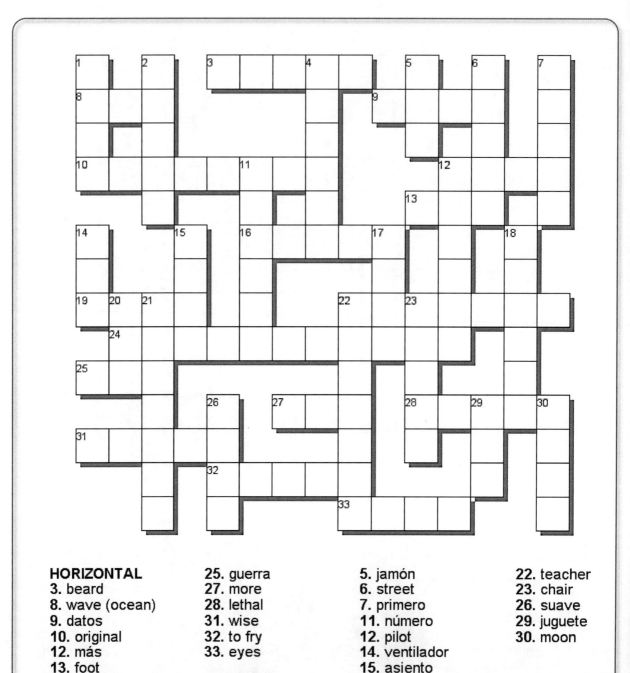

HORIZONTAL
3. beard
8. wave (ocean)
9. datos
10. original
12. más
13. foot
16. marzo
19. nape
22. mostaza
24. veterinarian

25. guerra
27. more
28. lethal
31. wise
32. to fry
33. eyes

VERTICAL
1. alone
2. patio
4. to dance

5. jamón
6. street
7. primero
11. número
12. pilot
14. ventilador
15. asiento
17. hora
18. piranha
20. grape
21. brain

22. teacher
23. chair
26. suave
29. juguete
30. moon

BONUS – BUSCAPALABRAS #1

a	c	e	r	a	c	e	i	t	e	s	t	a	f	a
g	e	s	p	o	s	a	s	e	m	a	n	a	l	d
u	l	c	i	c	a	t	r	i	z	c	a	l	l	e
j	e	o	a	l	e	c	a	t	o	r	c	e	h	c
a	s	b	f	r	e	s	a	s	i	e	n	t	o	i
r	t	a	b	v	p	c	p	s	l	m	d	a	n	r
q	e	o	a	a	c	i	h	u	p	a	u	m	g	c
u	c	l	h	m	h	a	n	u	m	a	r	í	o	o
i	l	l	o	p	o	í	j	t	g	a	a	g	c	e
t	e	a	r	o	c	j	a	ó	e	a	z	d	o	n
e	c	m	r	l	o	u	r	m	n	r	n	a	r	t
c	h	a	a	l	l	e	t	a	i	d	o	l	o	r
t	e	r	r	a	a	v	e	g	i	g	u	a	n	a
o	d	i	e	n	t	e	s	i	d	r	o	g	a	d
g	r	a	n	d	e	s	f	a	r	m	a	c	i	a

Palabras

aceite	asiento	circo	escoba	largo
acera	bahía	cobre	esposas	leche
aguja	cajón	corona	espuma	lechuga
ahorrar	calle	crema	estafa	llamar
amigo	carpintero	decir	farmacia	llave
ampolla	caspa	diente	fresa	magia
amígdala	catorce	dolor	grande	semana
arquitecto	celeste	droga	hongo	semanal
artes	chocolate	durazno	iguana	
	cicatriz	entrada	jueves	

BONUS – BUSCAPALABRAS #2

```
d  i  s  f  r  a  z  a  d  a  n  c  h  o  a
e  s  p  u  m  a  l  a  m  b  r  e  s  n  c
s  c  g  a  l  l  o  b  u  e  n  o  i  a  u
i  c  a  n  o  a  r  e  n  a  t  t  h  d  e
e  g  u  b  m  a  r  t  e  s  r  c  e  a  r
r  s  e  ñ  r  j  u  l  i  o  a  o  r  r  d
t  c  t  l  a  a  u  h  c  h  b  s  m  t  o
o  a  a  ó  a  d  c  g  g  a  a  t  a  e  f
r  j  l  l  m  t  o  a  u  r  r  a  n  s  l
i  ó  u  l  i  a  i  o  c  e  a  r  o  c  e
g  n  m  e  a  d  g  n  s  h  t  n  e  e  c
i  u  i  n  g  e  a  o  a  a  o  e  e  r  h
n  e  n  o  u  o  b  d  l  i  b  r  o  r  a
a  v  i  f  j  m  a  g  o  s  t  o  r  o  o
l  e  o  c  a  l  o  r  a  h  o  r  r  o  s
```

Palabras	artes	cebolla	flecha	julio
acuerdo	barato	cerro	frazada	libro
agosto	bueno	chistoso	~~fuego~~	lleno
aguja	cabra	cortina	gallo	martes
ahorros	cachorro	costa	gelatina	nadar
alambre	cajón	cuñado	granero	nueve
aluminio	calidad	desierto	hacha	original
ambos	calor	disfraz	hermano	sabor
anchoa	canoa	espuma	juego	
arena	carrera	estómago	juguete	

Una Nota del Autor / A Note from the Author:

Para cuando estés leyendo esta nota, habrás tenido la oportunidad de aumentar tu vocabulario español haciendo los crucigramas en este cuaderno.

Te agradezco *el esfuerzo y espero que, no solo hayas disfrutado del contenido pero también que lo hayas encontrado beneficioso.*

Es muy importante para mí saber tu opinión*. Si en caso quisieras comentar acerca del contenido de este cuaderno o necesitaras alguna explicación adicional, por favor, no vaciles en comunicarte conmigo.*

- - - - o - - - -

By the time you read this note, you will have had the opportunity to increase your Spanish vocabulary by doing the puzzles in this workbook.

I thank you *for the effort and hope you not only enjoyed the content but also found it beneficial.*

It is very important to me to receive your feedback*. If you would like to comment on the content of this book or need any additional explanation, please do not hesitate to contact me.*

C. E. Torreblanca
cesar@torreblanca.ca
www.torreblanca.ca

Mis Nuevas Palabras / My New Words:

This table is for you to write down all new words you learned after solving all crossword puzzles.
Esta tabla es para que escribas las palabras nuevas que aprendiste resolviendo los crucigramas.

Español	Inglés	M/F	Español	Inglés	M/F
[El] crucigrama	*[The] crossword*	*M*			
[La] manguera	*[The] hose*	*F*			

Español	Inglés	M/F	Español	Inglés	M/F

Español	Inglés	M/F	Español	Inglés	M/F

Clave de Respuestas:

Crucigrama #1

Crucigrama #2

Crucigrama #3

Crucigrama #4

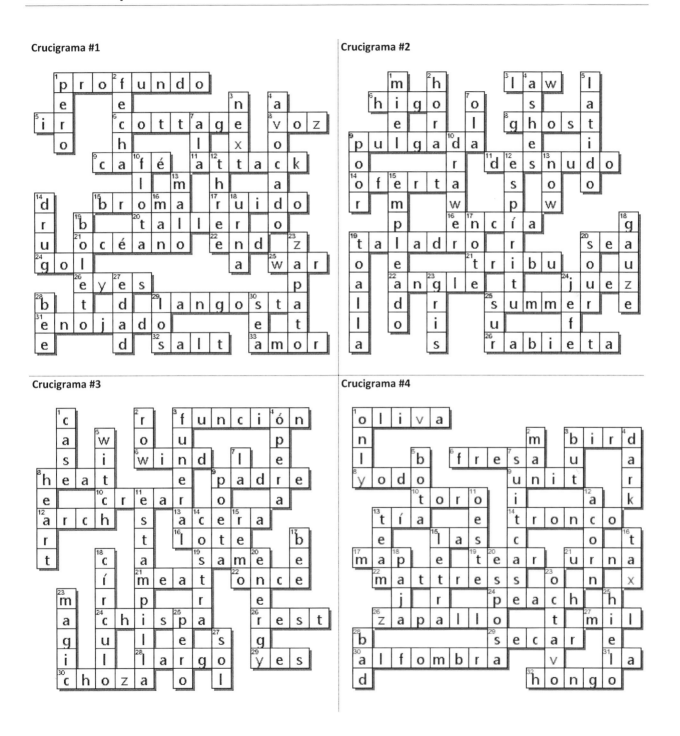

Crucigrama #5

Crucigrama #6

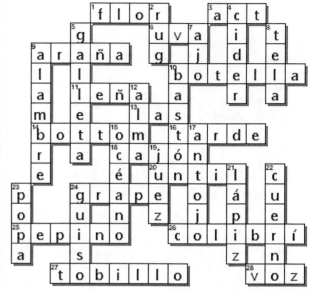

Crucigrama #7

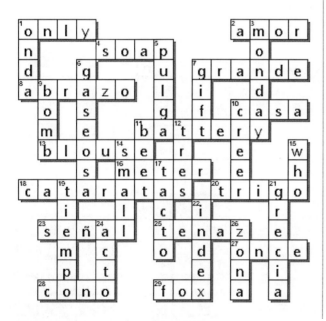

Crucigrama #8

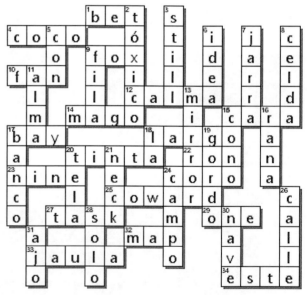

Crucigrama #9

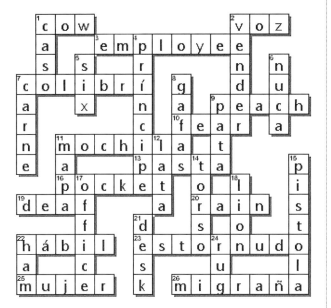

Crucigrama #10

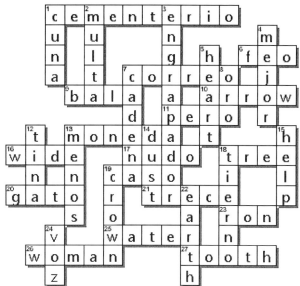

Crucigrama #11

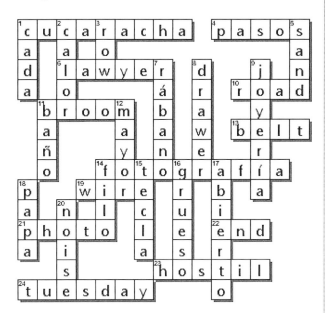

Crucigrama #12

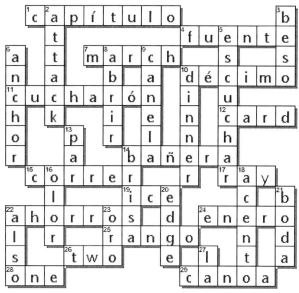

Crucigrama #13

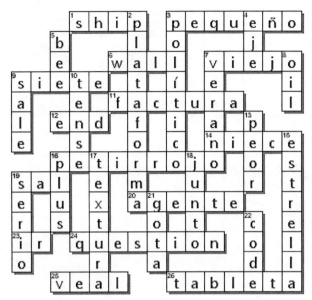

Crucigrama #14

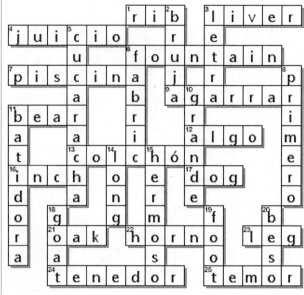

Crucigrama #15

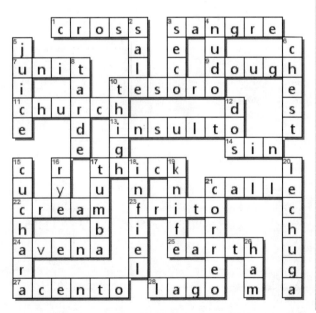

Crucigrama #16

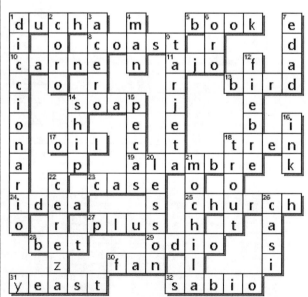

Crucigrama #17

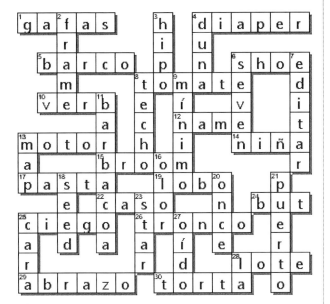

Crucigrama #18

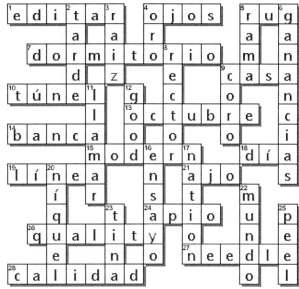

Crucigrama #19

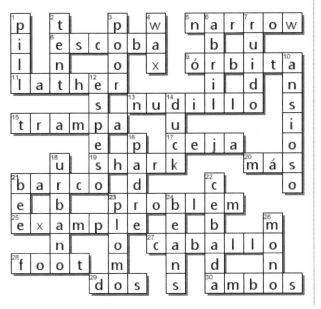

Crucigrama #20

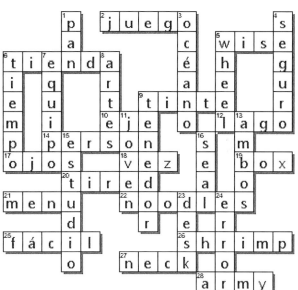

Crucigrama #21

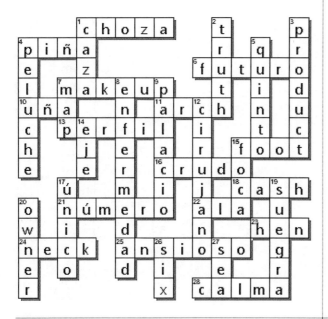

Crucigrama #22

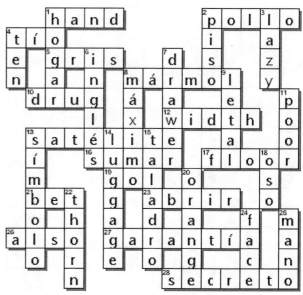

Crucigrama #23

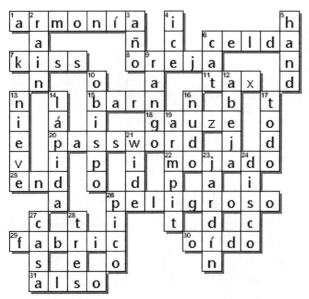

Crucigrama #24

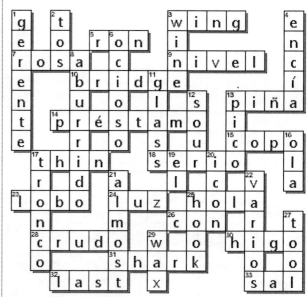

Crucigrama #25

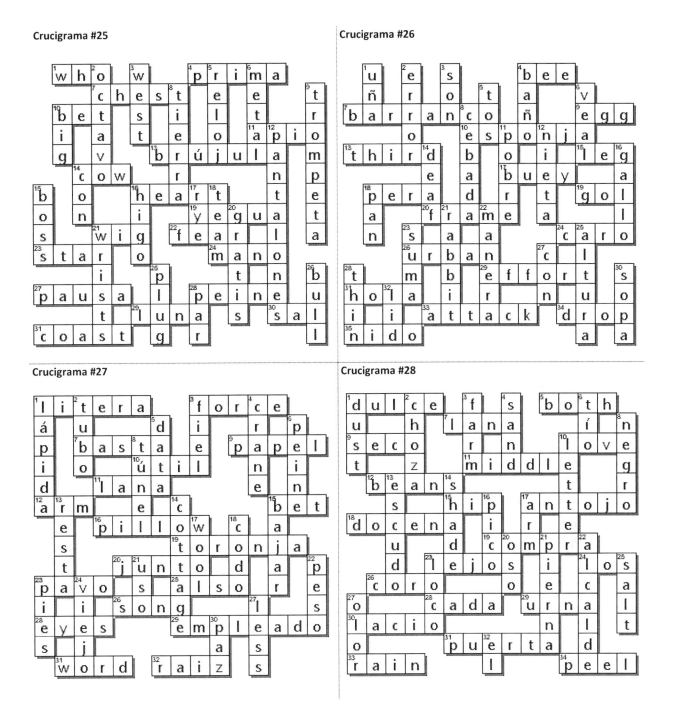

Crucigrama #26

Crucigrama #27

Crucigrama #28

Crucigrama #29

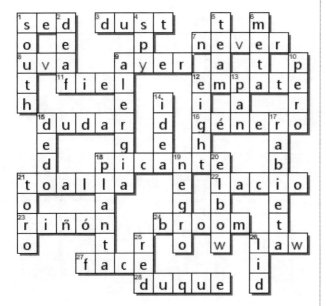

Crucigrama #30

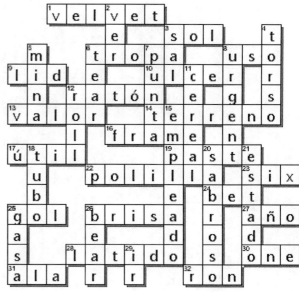

Crucigrama #31

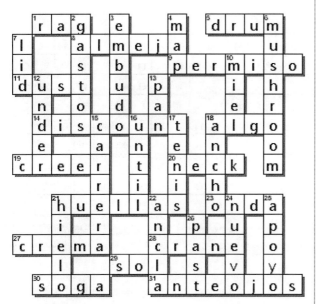

Crucigrama #32

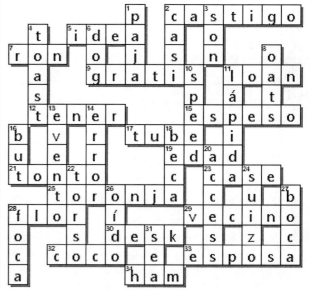

Crucigrama #33

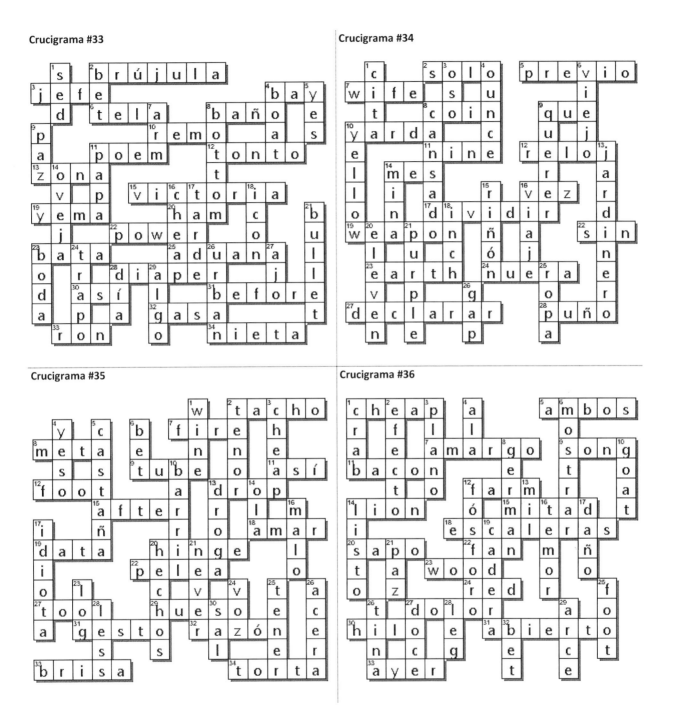

Crucigrama #34

Crucigrama #35

Crucigrama #36

Crucigrama #37

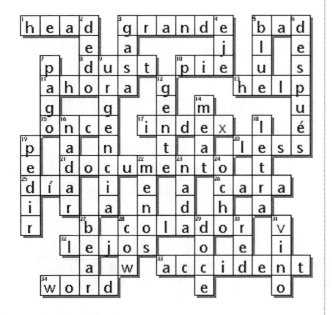

Crucigrama #38

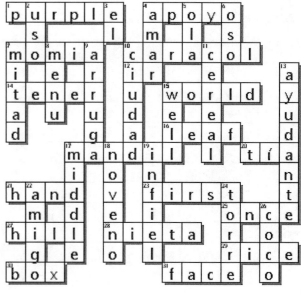

Crucigrama #39

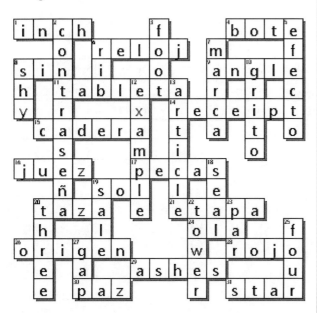

Crucigrama #40

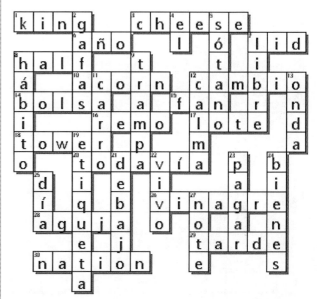

Crucigrama #41

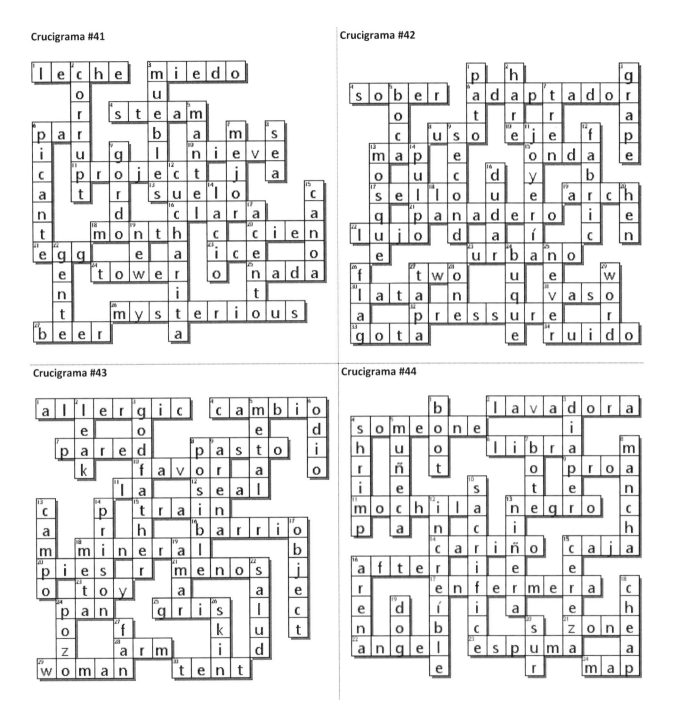

Crucigrama #42

Crucigrama #43

Crucigrama #44

Crucigrama #45

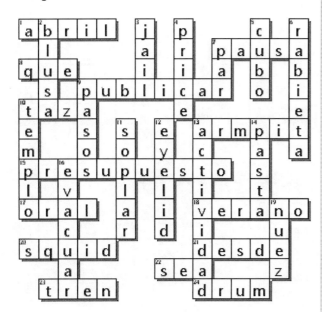

Crucigrama #46

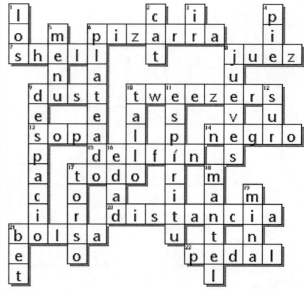

Crucigrama #47

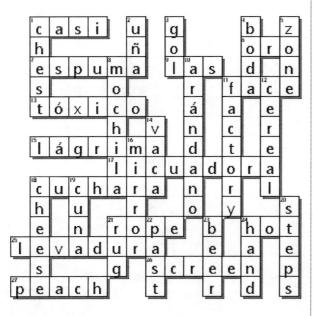

Crucigrama #48

Crucigrama #49

Crucigrama #50

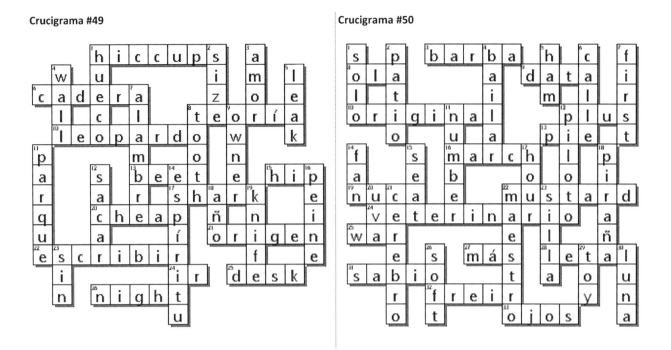

Mini #1

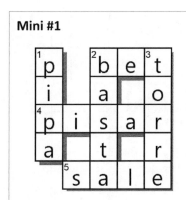

	¹p	²b	e	t	³t
	i	a			o
⁴p	i	s	a	r	
a		t			r
		⁵s	a	l	e

Mini #2

¹l	o	v	e	
e		²a		³n
⁴t	a	c	h	o
r		í		t
⁵a	h	o	r	a

Mini #3

¹l	o	²a	n	
u		l		³l
⁴j	u	i	c	e
o		ñ		ó
		⁵t	o	w	n

Mini #4

¹p		²s		³t
i		n		i
⁴s	t	a	i	n
t		k		t
⁵a	v	e	n	a

Mini #5

¹d	o	²g		³h
r		r		o
⁴o	d	i	a	r
g		t		n
⁵a	p	o	d	o

Mini #6

¹l	l	e	²n	o
i			u	
³m	u	j	e	r
i			v	
⁴t	e	n	e	r

Mini #7

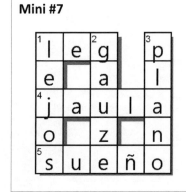

¹l	e	²g		³p
e		a		l
⁴j	a	u	l	a
o		z		n
⁵s	u	e	ñ	o

Mini #8

¹r	e	²s	t	
i		q		³h
⁴v	i	u	d	o
e		i		l
r		⁵d	í	a

Mini #9

¹e	m	²p	t	y
s		e		
³t	r	i	b	⁴u
e		n		s
		⁵y	e	s	o

Mini #10

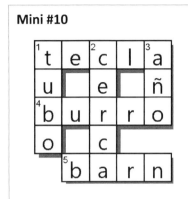

Mini #11

Mini #12

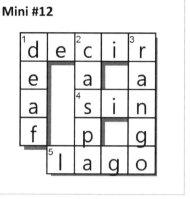

Mini #13

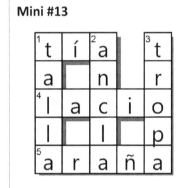

Mini #14

Mini #15

Mini #16

Mini #17

Mini #18

Mini #19

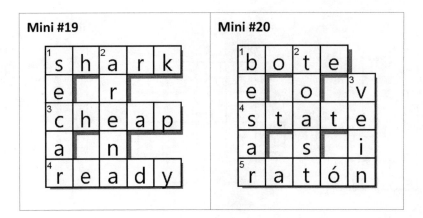

Mini #20

BONUS – Buscapalabras #1:

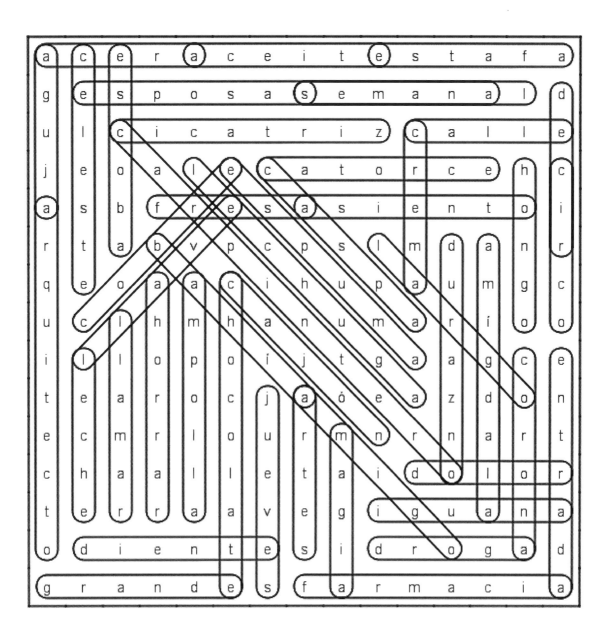

BONUS – Buscapalabras #2:

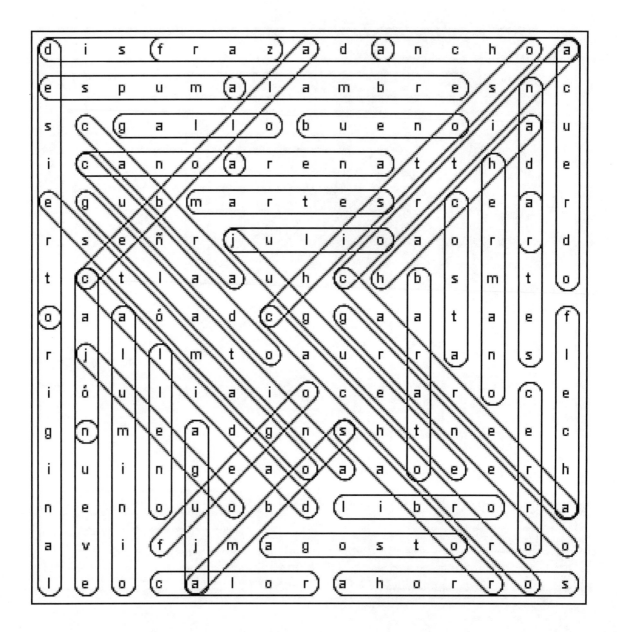

Made in United States
Orlando, FL
12 January 2025

57136554R00050